1

SHE BROKE HER NECK

2

THAT'S NOT WHAT I DID

1

HAVE YOU BEEN HERE BEFORE

2

NO THIS IS THE FIRST TIME OK....
THANK YOU VERY MUCH

ROBERT WILSON'S VISION

An exhibition of works by Robert Wilson
with a sound environment by Hans Peter Kuhn

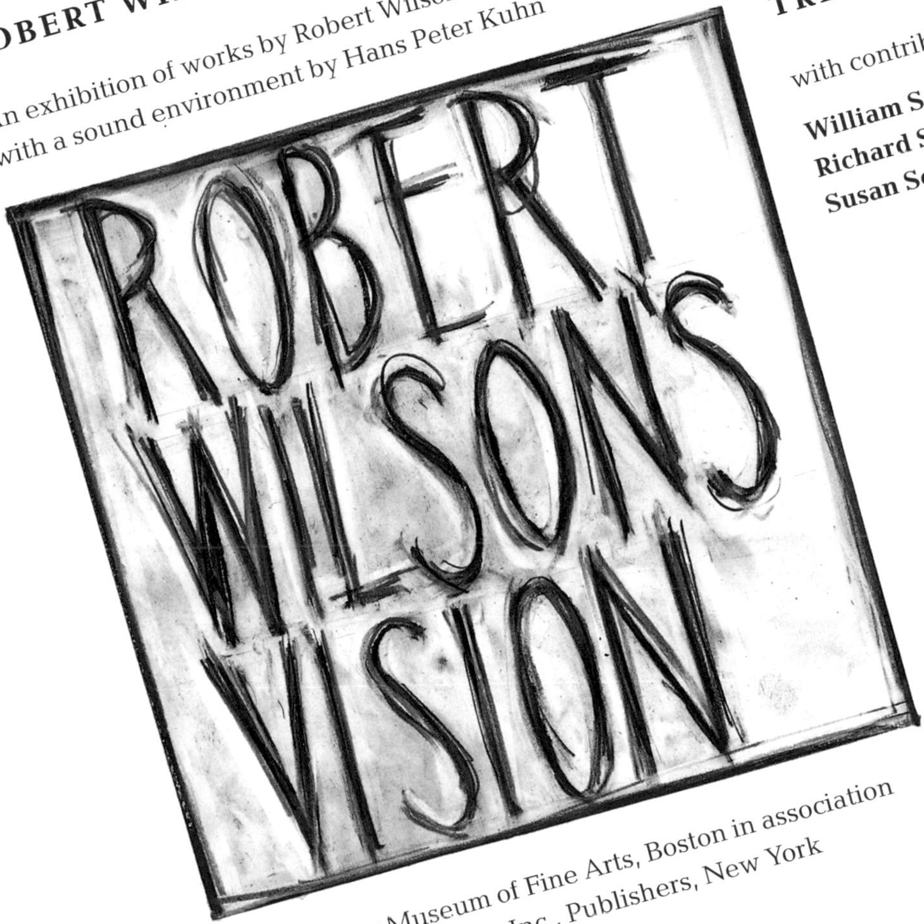

TREVOR FAIRBROTHER

with contributions by

William S. Burroughs
Richard Serra
Susan Sontag

Published by Museum of Fine Arts, Boston in association
with Harry N. Abrams, Inc., Publishers, New York

This exhibition was organized by the Museum of Fine Arts, Boston. It has been made possible by AT&T.

It is also supported by grants from the National Endowment for the Arts. Funding for the audio installation has been provided by the Lannan Foundation, Los Angeles.

The exhibition tour and dates:

Museum of Fine Arts, Boston
(February 6 – April 21)

Contemporary Arts Museum, Houston
(June 15 – August 18)

San Francisco Museum of Modern Art
(September 19 – December 1)

Printed in Germany

Copyright 1991 by the Museum of Fine Arts, Boston, Massachusetts
Library of Congress Catalogue Card no. 90-63761
ISBN 0-87846-324-0 (paper)
ISBN 0-8109-3959-2 (Abrams)

Designer: Carl Zahn
Color separations: System Repro, Filderstadt, Germany
Typesetter and printer: Dr. Cantz'sche Druckerei, Ostfildern, Germany
Binder: Lachenmaier, Reutlingen, Germany
Compact disc made by: Philips and Du Pont Optical Co.

Thanks to Freeman Dyson for permission to reprint quotation from *Primo Levi – Tullio Regge, Dialogo,* 1989; and to Suhrkamp Verlag, Frankfurt, Germany, for permission to reprint from Peter Weiss, *Notizbücher 1960–71,* entry of August 15, 1970; and to Alexander von Berswordt for permission to use the translation by Hunter G. Hannum.

Cover drawings by Robert Wilson, 1990.

Preliminary pages: Drawings for *A Letter for Queen Victoria,* 1973.
Paula Cooper Gallery, New York.

Frontispiece: Robert Wilson in performance of *A Letter for Queen Victoria,* 1974.
Photo by Pietro Privitera.

CONTENTS

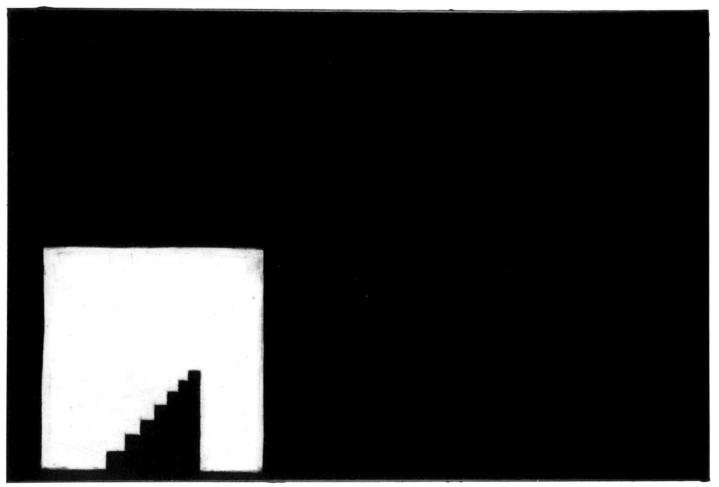

"ORLANDO"

Orlando: part 1, 1989
Drawing, 27 x 40 in.

Mr. and Mrs. William T. Solomon. Photo courtesy of Zozobra Fine Art, Inc.

Robert Wilson is widely acknowledged as one of the most creative forces in the art and theater of the last two decades. He has fused the roles of director and designer in a highly visual approach that gives formal independence to the elements of light, space, and sound. It is appropriate that an exhibition surveying Wilson's sculptures, drawings, videos, and installation works should originate in Boston. In 1985 the American Repertory Theatre in Cambridge and Boston's Institute of Contemporary Art produced the United States premiere of one part of Wilson's multi-national epic, *the CIVIL warS*. Robert Brustein and A.R.T. have continued to bring Wilson's work here, and it is becoming well known to Boston audiences.

Trevor Fairbrother conceived and organized this exhibition project. With the appointment of Kathy Halbreich as the first Beal Curator of Contemporary Art in 1988, and Trevor Fairbrother's appointment as associate curator in that department, planning for the project accelerated. Kathy Halbreich oversaw the complicated network of collaborations this unusual project accelerated. Together they oversaw the complicated network of collaborations this unusual project has required, and Trevor Fairbrother wrote the excellent and insightful catalogue, soliciting along the way contributions from William S. Burroughs, Richard Serra, and Susan Sontag.

A Robert Wilson exhibition is not quite like anything that has gone before it: perhaps this will be most notable in the case of the sound environment by Hans Peter Kuhn, based largely on the compositions he has created for several of Wilson's theater works of the last twelve years. Carl Zahn has designed a remarkably innovative catalogue that incorporates Kuhn's audio score in compact disc format.

I express my deepest thanks to all those institutions, galleries, and private individuals who have lent to this exhibition. This is a risk-taking but highly imaginative project. I am grateful to the National Endowment for the Arts and the Lannan Foundation for their support, and most especially to AT&T for its sponsorship of the exhibition and the national tour.

In particular, I would like to thank the Paula Cooper Gallery, and my colleagues Suzanne Delchanty, director of the Contemporary Arts Museum, Houston, and John R. Lane, director of the San Francisco Museum of Modern Art.

Robert Wilson's artistic vision is rich and complex: most important it breaks artificial barriers and promotes a spirit of free exchange and collaboration between different fields and media. With its fresh and creative approach to installation it may point to ways in which museums in general can benefit from contemporary art.

ALAN SHESTACK

Director, Museum of Fine Arts, Boston

ACKNOWLEDGMENTS

This project grew slowly and steadily for five years, and I am most grateful to the Museum of Fine Arts for providing such a lengthy and generous opportunity to work with Robert Wilson. And I am equally grateful to Robert Wilson for his characteristic patience, bolstered by his strong affection for this city. Hans Peter Kuhn's sounds have touched me emotionally for several years, and I am thrilled to have this opportunity to feature his work with Wilson. All those who have lent to the exhibition or who kindly gave me access to their collections deserve great thanks. At the Museum of Fine Arts I am indebted to Alan Shestack and Kathy Halbreich for their belief in and support of this venture. Kathy has been endlessly creative and encouraging about ways to proceed, whether financially, bureaucratically, philosophically, or artistically. In the preparation of the exhibition there are many other people to thank at the Museum: Theodore E. Stebbins, Jr., John Moors Cabot Curator of American Paintings, was an early supporter of the project; within the Department of Contemporary Art, curatorial assistant Catherine Modica, department assistant Susan Dimmock, and NEA intern Kathryn Potts were enormously helpful, as was Barrett Tilney in the Department of Paintings; Desirée Caldwell and Amy White administered the planning of the exhibition; Janet Spitz and Martha Reynolds supervised the fundraising activities; Linda Thomas and Pat Loiko coordinated the logistics within the Registrar's Office; Joan Norris and Linda Patch supervised the publicity. In the Education Department, I would like to thank Bill Burback, Joan Harlow and Barbara Martin. Tom Wong and Judith Downes in the Design Department have brought Wilson's ideas for the exhibition to fruition in the galleries; Mark Wise and Chris Hatch-field have worked equally successfully to realize Hans Peter Kuhn's sound environment. Sally Keeler and the staff of the Facilities Department must be congratulated on the difficult job of staging and installing the art.

The exhibition could not have been realized without the collaboration and creativity of Alan P. Symonds and Vicki Peterson of the American Repertory Theatre, who devised and supervised the fabrication of the most complicated components of the installation. Jonathan Miller and Max Leventhal were also key contributors at A.R.T. For their technical advice in the treatment or handling of the works of art I am most grateful to Arthur Beale, Jean-Louis Lachevre, Elizabeth Lunning, Michael Morano, Annette Manick, and Roy Perkinson. At the Museum School I want to give particular thanks to Lelia Amalfitano, director of exhibitions and visiting artists, for inviting Wilson to give a memorable public lecture in January 1988. Hans Peter Kuhn's stay in Boston during the installation was made possible with the support of the Visiting Artists Program of the Massachusetts College of Art; in particular I would like to thank Michele Furst.

I thank William S. Burroughs, Richard Serra, and Susan Sontag for their unique contributions to the book. This book about Robert Wilson would have been impossible without the help of his staff at the Byrd Hoffman Foundation: Mindi Dickstein, Dennis Redmond, and Ronald Vance have been tireless providers of information, photographs, and written materials, to say nothing of advice. Similarly, Wilson's dealer, Paula Cooper and her staff have been enormously helpful; in particular I want to thank Julie

Graham, who worked closely with me and the artist in selecting and locating works. I was most fortunate to have the help of two remarkable volunteers when preparing my research: Virginia Abblitt, who is now librarian at the School of the Museum of Fine Arts, Boston, and Peter Barr, a graduate student in art history at Boston University. Bonnie Porter was my invaluable colleague in our William Morris Hunt Memorial Library. Janice Sorkow, director of Photographic Services, and her staff deserve special thanks; Tom Lang's beautiful transparencies of several objects and drawings enormously enhance this publication. Carl Zahn's enthusiastic involvement is fully evident in the book he has created; he worked closely with me and Wilson in conceptualizing his design. I am especially grateful to Cynthia Purvis, also in the Office of Publications, for her skillful editing and advice. At Abrams Paul Gottlieb and Margaret Kaplan must be thanked for challenging us all to make the book as unusual as Robert Wilson's theater. Freeman Dyson graciously allowed us permission to reprint a quotation from *Primo Levi – Tullio Regge, Dialogo,* and Helene Ritzerfeld of Suhrkamp Verlag kindly permitted us to reprint a lengthy excerpt from Peter Weiss's *Notizbücher.* Barbara and Markus Hartmann and Klaus Prokop ably guided the book through production in Stuttgart and are arranging for copublishing a German edition.

Finally I express my thanks to a variety of people who helped me along the way: Steve Berkowitz, Robert Brustein, Lucinda Childs, Suzanne Delehanty, Richard Feigen, Reddi Ford, Jan Geidt, Seth Goldstein, Marion Goodman, Regina Guhl, Fred Jahn, Jeffrey Keough, Lance Kinz, John Kirk, Harold Leeds, Gillian Levine, R. Z. Manna, Ross Miller, Trina McKeever, Robert Orchard, Andrew Richards, Bob Riley, Paul Schmidt, Tina Summerlin, Lucien Terras, Annemarie Verna, Steve Wolfe, and Thomas Woodruff.

TREVOR FAIRBROTHER

Acting Curator, Department of Contemporary Art

15

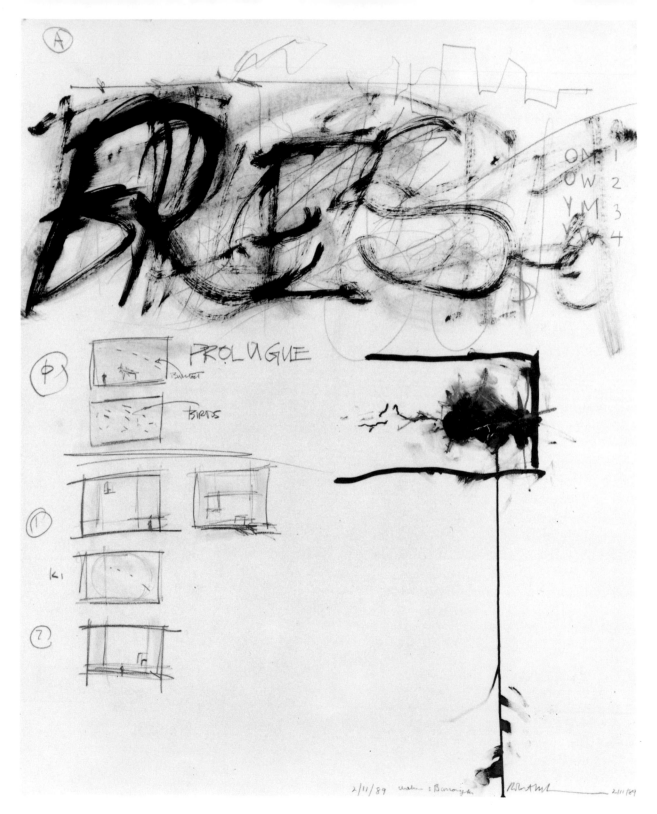

Bullet / Birds, 1989, William S. Burroughs and Robert Wilson. Drawing, 40 x 32 in.

ROBERT WILSON
by William S. Burroughs

Robert Wilson is primarily concerned with beauty – which implies, in certain quarters, escapism. And why should escapism carry an opprobious connotation? Are life boats and fire escapes to be shunned as Escapist?

Recent dream research has demonstrated that dreams are a *biological necessity*. No matter how much dreamless sleep the experimental subject (animal or human) is allowed, if his REM – that is, dream sleep – is consistently interrupted, he will soon show all the symptoms of sleeplessness: irrationality, lack of concentration, hallucinations and *eventual death*. Robert Wilson is presenting beautiful life-saving dream images on stage and canvas.

Working with Robert Wilson on *The Black Rider*, I was constantly impressed by his visionary grasp of the complex medium of opera. He sees what he wants, and is able to translate his inner vision into stage terms, and to circumvent the crippling conventions of dramatic presentation: what he calls 'ping pong dialogue' and soap opera plots.

The future of drama and opera rides with Robert Wilson.

Parsifal (Act 1), 1984
Drawing, 29¾ x 41½ in.
Paula Cooper Gallery, New York. Photo by Geoffrey Clements.

A PARSIFAL
by Susan Sontag
1990

Parzival, 1987, Drawing, 23¼ x 29 in.
John-Erik Bergamus. Photo by Best Fotografie.

Scene 1. A landscape (the dark forest, the lake, the tears). Garden gnomes. A column of light.

YOUNG MAN.	I am Parsifal. Here, they say, time becomes space.
OSTRICH.	I said it. I was once an expert explainer. Now I watch.
YOUNG MAN.	I'm passing through.
OSTRICH.	You watch.

(Enter **KING OF PAIN** on a motorized gurney, naked under a gauze sheet, an oxygen feed strapped to his face.)

KING OF PAIN.	Pain. Blood. Semen. Tears. The wound. I am open. I am guilty. I will die.

(Borne slowly across stage, right to left; exits.)

YOUNG MAN.	Oh.
OSTRICH.	Does that hurt your heart.
YOUNG MAN.	I don't know.
OSTRICH.	I'm sure you have some feelings despite the evident barbarism of your upbringing.
YOUNG MAN.	I'm not good at talking. Perhaps I am retarded.
OSTRICH.	You won't win my sympathy that way.
YOUNG MAN.	No really I am a very simple person. I have never known the need to be different. Should I be different.
OSTRICH.	You expect something from me, something parental perhaps.
YOUNG MAN.	I don't know.
OSTRICH.	But your name is Parsifal.
YOUNG MAN.	I don't know. I say things and then I don't remember them.
OSTRICH.	Once I explained. But I have changed. The explanations died. I have more to learn than to impart.
YOUNG MAN.	What is… died.
OSTRICH.	Foolish boy. What is *that*. (Points to Uzi slung over **YOUNG MAN's** shoulder.) You try my patience.
YOUNG MAN.	Oh this. It's nothing. In my country everyone has one.

(Enter **TWO KNIGHTS** in black armor, their vizors down, bearing dead swan on a stretcher.)

KNIGHT 1.   You have violated our law Parsifal.

YOUNG MAN.   I was mistaken. I don't know my name. Why does everyone know my name. I don't know who I am. I claim the position of innocence. Of ignorance.

KNIGHT 2.   (Removing his helmet) Parsifal you have violated our laws.

YOUNG MAN.   Of ignorance. Of innocence.

(Takes Uzi and aims it at **KNIGHT 2**.)

          And in a moment, when you'll be on the ground with holes in your body and —

(Enter **KUNDRY**, wide-eyed, hair streaming.)

KUNDRY.   Stop Parsifal. Your flight from feeling has ended. Time to grieve. Your mother is dead.

(**YOUNG MAN** collapses on the ground. **KNIGHTS 1 and 2** confiscate Uzi and exit.)

          (Laughs bitterly) Yes that is how I thought he would react.

OSTRICH.   Let him be, Kundry. He has a shining future.

YOUNG MAN.   (Weeps) Mother mother my sweet mother. So this is death.

(**KUNDRY** leans over, kisses him on the brow.) Yes my heart hurts now.

OSTRICH.   It is happening. It is beginning. I am proud. (Pause) Don't be weak. There is no consolation. But I am watching.

(**KUNDRY** helps **YOUNG MAN** to his feet.)

(To **KUNDRY**) Let the boy be! (To **YOUNG MAN**) It used to be thought that the ostrich hatches her eggs by gazing on them, and if she suspends her gaze for even a minute the eggs are addled.

YOUNG MAN.	Is that like the fairy tales my mother would tell me. Oh my mother. (Leans against **KUNDRY**) Oh my heart.
OSTRICH.	Utmost unremitting unrelenting unflagging undiluted concentration is required. Never forget. Never lose sight. Every minute a concentrated one. Count.(Pause) Further we are told that if an egg is bad the ostrich will break it.
KUNDRY.	Don't moralize. You're confusing the lad. He comes from another time. No one cares about the old stories, the old push and pull of good and evil. They only knew the names. Some famous glittering names.
OSTRICH.	This is why in Eastern Orthodox churches ostrich eggs are often suspended from the ceiling. As the ostrich will break an addled egg, so will God deal with evil people.
KUNDRY.	Don't be vindictive. All my life I have suffered from the vindictiveness of the just.
YOUNG MAN.	My mother…
KUNDRY.	But look at our boy our Parsifal. You'd let him faint. I will bring him water.

(Exits.)

OSTRICH.	Much has happened. Don't listen to that whore. You have a great destiny before you. I am watching. Do you know what you have witnessed.
YOUNG MAN.	I don't know.
OSTRICH.	Watch again.

(Re-enter **KING OF PAIN** on gurney, groaning and holding his side.)

KING OF PAIN.	I'm bleeding. I'm guilty. Will no one drink me. Oh… (Crosses stage very slowly, left to right; exits.)
OSTRICH.	Well?
YOUNG MAN.	Sometimes I think I understand.
OSTRICH.	Now? Is it now?
YOUNG MAN.	And my understanding copies itself, multiplies like the stars. It

	dives skyward like a dolphin. (Pauses.) But then... I don't know.
OSTRICH.	It's time for your press conference.

(Enter **ONE HUNDRED KNIGHTS** in black armor, most with faces covered.)

YOUNG MAN.	I have very little to say. Where is Kundry.
A KNIGHT	You may say whatever you like. Expectations are low now.
YOUNG MAN.	No I would like to make sense. I don't seek every liberty.
OSTRICH.	Go slowly. Remember the ostrich.
ANOTHER KNIGHT.	Don't humor him. (They seize **YOUNG MAN** and drag him off-stage.)

Scene 2. Grail Hall. Huge oval steel table. Giant egg suspended from ceiling.

YOUNG MAN.	There are some personal questions I may decline to answer. (**KNIGHTS**, who are standing behind the table, bang their helmets impatiently. One comes forward and hands **YOUNG MAN** a microphone, rat-grey.)
	May I have a chair. Please.
	   (Another brings a chair.)
	Thank you.
	   (Sits.)

OSTRICH.	(To audience, from his high perch near egg) I was impressed by his beautiful manners. They were not the manners you would expect of someone from his uncouth background.

(Enter **KUNDRY** with a glass of water.)

	Eternal returns.
YOUNG MAN.	Thanks.
KUNDRY.	You don't have to thank Kundry. No one thanks Kundry.
YOUNG MAN.	How unfair. (Sighs) But it is not my intention to challenge how things are done here. I am here not to alter existing arrangements but to exalt them. I am extremely ignorant. I read as little as possible. I trust what I feel. I am a very spontaneous person.

(Enter **KLINGSOR**, naked except for a loin bib.)

KLINGSOR   Kundry help him. As only you can do.
KUNDRY.   (raising finger to lips) Shhhhhh...
                     (**YOUNG MAN** raises microphone high in the air. It turns red.
                     Everyone falls silent. He brings it to his lips.)
YOUNG MAN.   Yes, I've been stalling and, yes, I'm ready to begin. (Stops,
                     suddenly gripped by a fierce pain. Takes a deep breath, starts
                     again.) Yes, I didn't understand that it was wrong to kill the
                     swan. I was raised to love weapons. I was raised in a violent
                     country. I was a body. Body always moving, even when still. I
                     took aim, I fired. My mother sent me forth. I was in the
                     landscape. Moving swiftly. Then I saw the old man being borne
                     on a litter. I discovered slowness, sadness. Yes, I was sad. And,
                     yes, I threw down my weapon. They taught me shame. Yes, I'm
                     sorry now. Yes, they said I was simple. Then, perhaps too easily,
                     they said I was holy. Yes, I've been told that silly once meant
                     holy. No, I don't think I understood. They mentioned the Grail,
                     which I thought was a person, so I asked, Who is the Grail. They
                     laughed, I was exasperating. It seems funny now, yes. They
                     said I would find out if I could find out, if I was the chosen one.
                     I was on my own. I have to become someone else. (Pauses)
                     More water.

(**KUNDRY** hands him another glass.)

                     Thank you very much.
                     (Drinks.)
                     No, of course, it didn't start out that way. I really couldn't talk.
                     No, I wasn't pretending. No, I was innocent. Yes, I was
                     ignorant. No, that's something I can't know. No, I don't see
                     myself like that. No, that's too personal. No, it wasn't a mission.
                     It just happened. It's not my job to explain. My shyness, yes,
                     how can you expect me to comment on that. There wasn't any.
                     We were poor, the birds sang, we festooned the mountain slope

with candles. Never, no, that never seemed to bother anyone. I can't explain but it didn't surprise me, no. I looked, I listened, I saw light everywhere, it was dark in my heart. I found what was meticulous in the radiance. I was fragile, I was emphatic. Everyone gathered around me, they wanted me to transform them. I was usually late. They waited. I didn't speak. They drew closer. When they asked me I said I didn't know. And yes, I did know, know that not speaking, withholding information, confers great power. I took responsibility for everyone, I took responsibility for no one. They were a group, yes, a community, yes, of yearning, they were lost, they wanted to be saved. I didn't say I would save anyone, how could you imagine that, but they attributed these powers to me, and yes, they did feel like my powers, and they changed their lives for me, they were there when I needed them, for our common purpose, for our sumptuous rituals, and I was a leader. But, yes, I didn't want to be a leader. They didn't want to see my wound. (Pause) I didn't want, and that was my strength, and they wanted me, yes, and I tried to stay still. I tried to keep moving. Moving slower now. Moving slowly, so as not to disturb the picture. I want the picture to last.

(Grimaces. Seems faint. Forces himself to stand.)

No, I'm all right. Yes, a wall of words. I didn't think about it. They wanted a barbarian. They wanted a beautiful youth. I didn't speak. I let them do what they wanted. I controlled everything. They stared at me. I was tender, I was ruthless. I was compassionate, I was indifferent. I smiled sweetly. It would work either way. They did the best they could. I took a vacation. I wrote postcards. I came back. They were waiting. How could I know that it wouldn't matter what I did. I stayed up all night. They organized everything. But in my name, yes, of course. It was an institution. They told me they wanted me to do my best. I did my best. I did more. Sometimes they knew better than I.

Yes, I let them. Why not, it was me they knew better than I.
(Sinks back in chair.)
One thing followed another. Slowly.

KLINGSOR.	(Jeering) And what's that between your legs, are you going to cut it off. It has a mind of its own too.

YOUNG MAN.	Money sex drugs limousines. No, I don't deny my relationship with Kundry. Who says I had no impure feelings, I don't. The living ichor. Psychotic normality. The young got older. I worked hard I thought I deserved to relax. I went out and let myself caress and be caressed in the park, on the golf course, in the museum, in the private jet. Nothing was happening. Everything was still. I caught a plane. I saw the ship soldered to the horizon. I went to Kundry's house. After the party, yes, it was late. I saw the squad car parked out in front with its cherry flashing. I sneaked in the back door. Of course I'm being honest now. Why wouldn't I be honest.

OSTRICH.	(To audience, from his perch) He is still somewhat naive. He's telling you that he feels that wound.

YOUNG MAN.	I desired Kundry. (Pause) Many people have desired me. (Pause) I didn't have the time. I made it go very slowly. She died at my feet. (KUNDRY sinks to floor, dead.) I would not love her. I let her die at my feet.

(Exit some **KNIGHTS**, who return with scaffold on wheels. **YOUNG MAN** mounts it very slowly as hc continues talking.) This is a play, this is a death, this is slowness. If we slow down enough we will never die. (Reaches top of scaffold.) If we move, we move into the future. We will die.

(Remains motionless. Lights up.)
We will not die.

Black-out. Curtain.

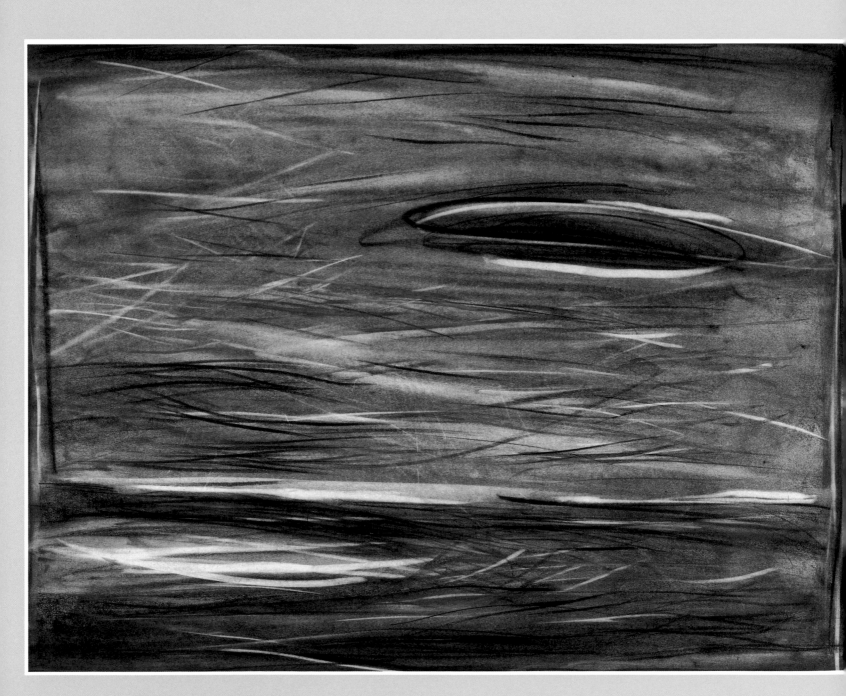

Parzival, 1987
Drawing, 22½ x 28½ in.

Paula Cooper Gallery, New York. Photo by Museum of Fine Arts, Boston.

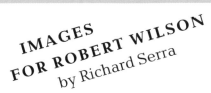

IMAGES FOR ROBERT WILSON
by Richard Serra

There exists a tendency of the stars to evaporate, so that 10 percent of the stars will leave the galaxy. The spiraling arms of the galaxy will end by disappearing; the nucleus of the galaxy will become ever denser, a gigantic black hole being formed at its center. All around there will be very many black holes, due to the collapse of various stars. All the stars catalyze to the point of becoming iron. If I take this dish and I leave it alone for an immense time, say 10^{30} years, it will first of all assume a spheric shape, because the reciprocal force of gravity of the various parts of the object induces slow atomic transitions, due to which an atom moves ever closer to the object's center of mass. Over times that long, any object becomes practically liquid and takes on a spherical form: strictly speaking, solid objects do not exist. Over an even longer time, there is always a very small but finite probability of catalysis of thermo-nuclear reactions, by which contiguous but not superimposed nuclei of different atoms can fuse and produce iron with the release of energy. A body of this kind always develops a little energy, slowly converting itself into iron. Thus the universe is filling up with iron balls: the Moon becomes an iron billiard ball, and so do the Earth and the planets. These billiard balls will end by colliding with one another.

FREEMAN DYSON, quoted by Tullio Regge in *Primo Levi – Tullio Regge, Dialogo*, 1989.

In the morning, without really being aware of it, almost as a regular thing, we assume our places for a ritual commemoration of the dead. While we are supplying our body with the first nourishment of the day, we take in the reports in the newspapers, chewing, swallowing, we learn about those who have been massacred, dismembered, burnt to death, crushed, drowned, about those who have perished from disease, weakness, starvation or despair, about those who have been struck down individually, in couples, in small groups, all the way up to the masses, the uncounted numbers. The sites where these deaths occurred were street corners, hospitals, offices, living rooms, factories, gathering places, means of transportation on land, on water, in the air, they lay in churned up earth, under spring tides and in the wake of sudden tempests, in deserts filled with stillness, in the midst of terrible turbulence. Unexpectedly, from behind your back, the end came, or washed over someone whose eyes were still wide open, it lunged at you out of a doorway, in an alley, knife thrusts ripped you to pieces, revolver bullets pulverized your skull, clubs beat you to the ground, or it was only a hard flat hand that struck your throat. Still half asleep at our morning memorial service we read of those centers where the slaughter is concentrated, in certain cities people are dying in increasing quantities, here the extermination has been recorded statistically, with the aid of tables we can compare the number of those who have been stabbed and blown up with last month's, last year's number, and the visions in which these moments are captured become more and more drastic, and our morning meal begins to merge with the slit open bellies, the ripped out intestines, the cut off heads, the handwriting on the wall written in the blood of the murder victims. At great length and with a growing wealth of detail, the descriptions of the murderers' trials are becoming increasingly cold and casual, we don't even notice this any more as we read them, we are already acquainted with this numbness, are already acquainted with this total incomprehension of guilt, already understand the indignation of the condemned who can't grasp, who can never admit, that the lives of others have been snuffed out at their hands, after all they were only carrying out what a legitimate mechanism decreed, what was ordered from above, over them were always the big institutions that had taught them to choke, to strangle, to beat up, to pull the trigger, here we read that someone did away with a dozen, that wasn't so many, the orders always concerned much larger numbers, here someone was made responsible for the death of hundreds, even thousands, there someone had been involved in the liquidation of ten thousand, of a hundred thousand, and sometimes you read, after all this occurred decades ago, this has no meaning anymore because since that time hundreds of thousands, millions, have been wiped out with impunity in similar fashion, and we don't even get dizzy at the figures that stand for lifeless bodies, millions of lifeless mouths and eyes, and we do not balk at the horror of corpses lying before us, for we have long been aware of the kind of world we live in, we are already so familiar with the everyday nature of lying, of massacres, of the crushing and burying of human bodies, of murderers going around scot-free, of the free rein of their henchmen, that we don't cry out, don't even groan, it's always the other people who have to face it, it can never happen to us, until you find out at first hand that one morning you came very close yourself to lying as rotting flesh on the breakfast table and having people spread your obituary on their rolls between the butter and the jam. No, not even this knowledge can rouse you out of your dazed state, you can't rush to the aid of even the most insignificant single death, your grief is not sufficient for even one grave, and the sight of the mass graves, your empathy with those tangled bodies, would tear you to pieces if you could grasp the phenomenon, the mere suspicion of it must be suppressed, for you have to think of selfpreservation, of going on with your miserable chewing and breathing for a few more minutes, for without this nourishment, without this appetite, without this sustenance of yourself you can't make any good resolutions at all, resolutions to remedy in some fashion the misery, the murdering, you have read so much on the subject, have already been involved with so many proposals for reform, have also already shown where you stand, have left no doubt about what you consider important, where you see your allies, where your enemies are, have made public proclamations, have marched along demonstrations, now you have to pamper yourself, regain your strength, take care of yourself, for still more is going to be required of you, still more expected of you, you are still going to be needed, while the others, far away, directly in front of you, fall down and grow stiff, while the presses of the mass murderers spew out their deception while madness increasingly distorts the faces of the supreme commanders-in-chief, stuff in your piece of bread, pour your coffee down your throat . . .

PETER WEISS, *Notizbücher 1960-1971*, entry of August 15, 1970; translation by Hunter G. Hannum.

Weight is a value for me, not that it is any more compelling than lightness, but I simply know more about weight than lightness and therefore I have more to say about it, more to say about the balancing of weight, the diminishing of weight, the addition and subtraction of weight, the concentration of weight, the rigging of weight, the propping of weight, the placement of weight, the locking of weight, the psychological effects of weight, the disorientation of weight, the disequilibrium of weight, the rotation of weight, the movement of weight, the directionality of weight, the shape of weight. I have more to say about the perceptual and meticulous adjustments of weight, more to say about the pleasure derived from the exactitude of the laws of gravity. I have more to say about the processing of the weight of steel, more to say about the forge, the rolling mill and the open hearth.

We are all restrained and condemned by the weight of gravity. However, Sisyphus pushing the weight of his boulder endlessly up the mountain does not catch me up as much as Vulcan's tireless labor at the bottom of the smoking crater, hammering out raw material. The constructive process, the daily concentration and effort appeal to me more than the light fantastic, more than the quest for the ethereal. Everything we choose in life for its lightness soon reveals its unbearable weight.

We face the fear of unbearable weight: the weight of repression, the weight of constriction, the weight of government, the weight of tolerance, the weight of resolution, the weight of responsibility, the weight of destruction, the weight of suicide, the weight of history which dissolves weight and erodes meaning to a calculated construction of palpable lightness. The residue of history: the printed page, the flicker of the image, always fragmentary, always saying something less than the weight of experience.

RICHARD SERRA, Summer 1988, Cape Breton

THE NIGHT BEFORE THE DAY

by Trevor Fairbrother

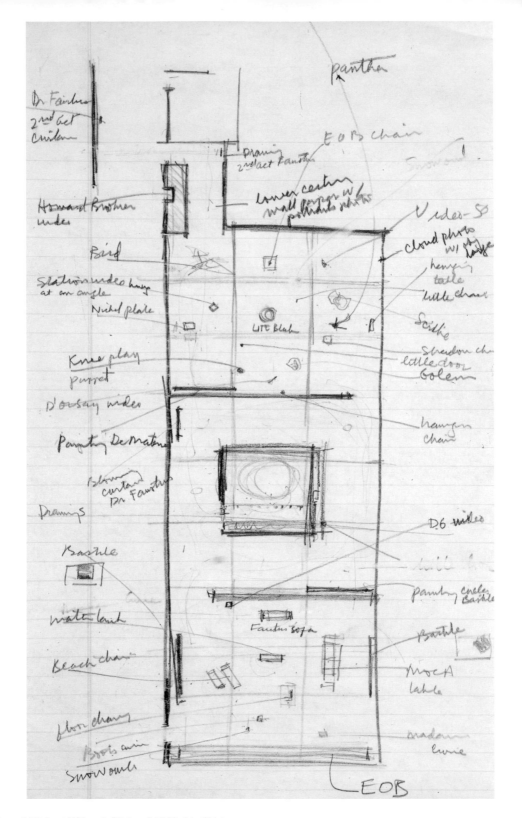

Plan for the installation of "Robert Wilson's Vision," 1989. 14 x 8½ in.

Museum of Fine Arts, Boston. Photo by Museum of Fine Arts, Boston.

In this exhibition Robert Wilson, with the help of the German sound artist Hans Peter Kuhn, refines the theatricality that is always a part of the viewer's museum experience. In keeping with the pluralist sensibility of the 1970s, when Wilson reached artistic maturity, his work has ranged restlessly and ambitiously in many directions – from the materially grounded, yet dramatic impressions of his drawings and sculptures to the fugitive stagings of form, light, sound, and movement created in his theater. Whether in design, the fine arts, or the theater, all of Wilson's activities disrupt the hierarchies that traditionally limit relationships between different art forms and means of expression. His gift as an inventor of haunting visions is undisputed; however, there is more to his work than the seductive impact of its presentation. The bittersweet, idiosyncratic beauty of his images should not obscure the fact of their ambivalent and sometimes painful content. The rapture in the work is constantly threatened or modified by apparent randomness, confusion, anxiety, discomforting sounds, and silences. His art can be as unsettling as it is enthralling, and the interplay between these various aspects makes Wilson's vision as rewarding to contemplate as it is pleasurable and cathartic to behold.

Wilson's personal energy, pragmatism, willfulness, and his well-publicized success have been greeted with awe, envy, boredom, and hostility. For some chroniclers of the avant garde the presentation of the Robert Wilson/Philip Glass opera *Einstein on the Beach* at New York's Metropolitan Opera House in 1976 boded an ominous alliance with the commercial world: it seemed to forecast the capitulation of alter-

native theater to mainstream institutional values. Since then Wilson has been an easy target for adherents to a strictly political, anti-establishment point of view. Recently he has come under the critical scrutiny of a new generation of theater directors, such as Peter Sellars, who are building in part on his contributions. In 1989 Sellars wrote: "For the last three hundred years or so, music has generally dominated what we now come to think of as the European operatic tradition… But at other times, and in other places, different elements have exerted their hegemony … In the age of Hollywood movies, television, and Robert Wilson, the image is a source of singular fascination. And I suspect that it is Hollywood movies, television, and Robert Wilson that have rendered theater temporarily obsolete and forced many of us who are interested in theater to take refuge in the realm of opera and redeem our tattered selves."[1] Sellars' first sentences in this same essay could, ironically, serve as a précis of twenty years of laudatory comments about Wilson's broadening and reinvention of theater's potential: "In an age when the interrelatedness of things is increasingly the issue, opera becomes the medium of choice. Multilingual, multicultural, multimedia, diachronic, dialogic, dialectical, and somehow strangely delectable, opera is the one form that seems to have a chance of reproducing and invoking the simultaneities, confusions, juxtapositions, bitter tragedy, and just plain malarkey that constitute the texture of recent history."

Theatricality is a given with Wilson, thus it is not surprising that this exhibition is hard to categorize in conventional museum terms. What could have been a routine retrospective of art objects made independently of his live performance activities eventually metamorphosed into a true collaboration. In August 1989, after three years of general discussion in Boston and elsewhere, the moment was suddenly right. Wilson spent a day at the Museum of Fine Arts studying the gallery, and our goal came clearly into focus. My desire to present a comprehensive selection of his works on paper, videos, furniture, costumes, sculpture, theater drops, and installation projects became his opportunity to make a new, short-lived art work on a large scale, inevitably mining the veins between artistic fields and media. The installation piece with a sound environment by Wilson's frequent collaborator on stage productions, Hans Peter Kuhn, would challenge theater's status quo, allowing the visitor an actor's access to a "stage" to explore a relatively static spectacle. A retrospective of not only Wilson's work but Kuhn's as well, the project also provided the occasion for a collaborative book, designed by Carl Zahn, that incorporated Kuhn's sounds in a re-mixed composition for compact disc.

Wilson frequently begins a new work for the theater with a simple modular or geometric diagram, which he subsequently reworks and elaborates during the development of the piece. In the case of the Boston exhibition, he examined the 15-foot-square coffered units that make up the ceiling of the Gund Gallery, and diagrammed the grid these squares defined. It was three units wide and nine units long, making the proportions of the floor plan one to three. Wilson plotted walls to divide the space into three square rooms (each comprising nine ceiling units). He saw the entry to the first room as a site for an introductory installation. Having derived what might be imagined

as a prologue and three acts, we plotted the exhibition, using index cards and photographs representing the principal objects.

By the end of the one-day visit Wilson had conceived of an exhibition that would unfold like a journey and suggest the passage of a day. His title for the work as a whole was *The Night before The Day*. Passing a television documentary about Wilson, the viewer would enter through a narrow corridor. The first room, spacious and bright, would feature objects (several of them suspended from the ceiling) suggestive of the fanciful flight of the youthful imagination. The middle room, gray, formal, and pivotal, would be densely hung with drawings of all sizes, and would house a smaller room in its center enclosing the bizarre installation piece, *Memory of a Revolution*. The third and last room, open like the first, would foster a contrasting mood with dark walls and an ominous ensemble of objects. Wilson summarized these ideas by sketching a plan of the space on a legal note pad.

The distinct divisions of this structure – entrance and three rooms – guided Hans Peter Kuhn in creating his four sound pieces. The exhibition's simple units give Wilson freedom to adapt the exhibition to the other museum sites where it will be installed. Five video works were originally intended to be integrated into the three large rooms. In order to prevent their soundtracks from undermining Kuhn's sound environments, and their televised images from interfering with the free flow of visitors through the spaces, the videos will be shown in a separate space adjoining the exit from Room III.

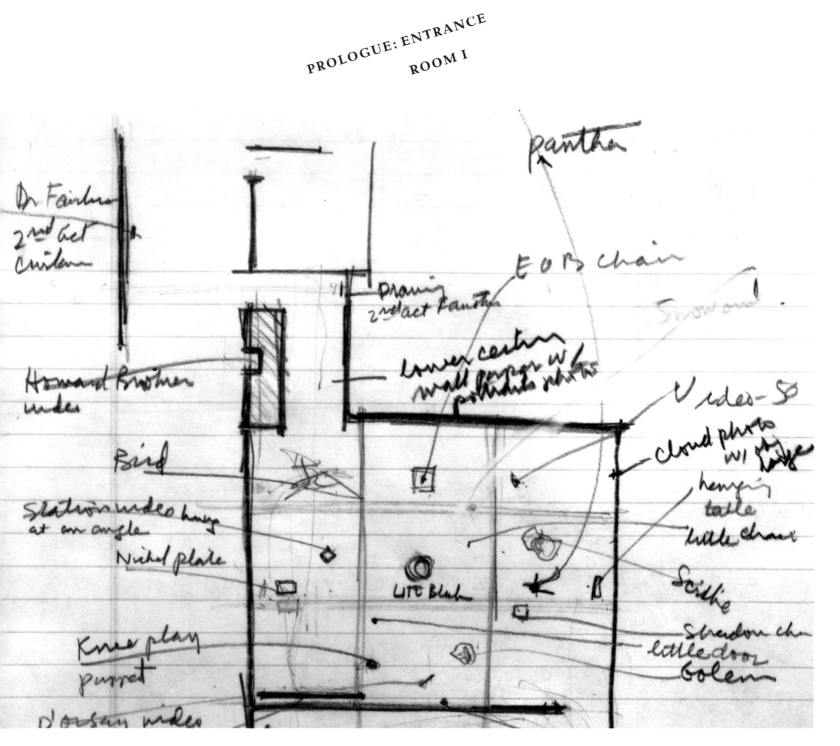

Detail of plan for the installation of "Robert Wilson's Vision," 1989

PROLOGUE: ENTRANCE

[Wilson] rejects that speed-up … which we accept as part of
the theater, and restores something of the pace of real time to
his world. Some things are very s-l-o-w but this does not
matter. At times it is like watching cloud formations, slowly
evolving their figurative suggestions, and at times, naturally
more rarely, it is like watching a street accident. This is visual
theater – you think of painters you might have known, and
forgotten animals from your youth. But there are also literary
memories as you wander rather comfortably through the landscape of Wilson's creation, pausing to ruminate, ponder or
wonder about it. It is theater that deliberately gives you time
to daydream. Indeed it is theater that has put a stop to time.[2]
Clive Barnes

At his lectures, Wilson stands silently at the podium before
speaking. When entering his performances, audiences usually
find some presence or activity already going on (an object
illuminated on the stage, or perhaps a performer seated in
silence). House lights dim slowly and in silence. The entrance
space or corridor of *The Night before The Day* creates a similar
sense of beginning, gently moving the visitor's body and mind
out of the public space of the museum into the threshold of
another place. The setting Wilson chose to evoke in this
boundary corridor is the forest: it holds a fascination for him,
since he grew up in the unwooded openness of central Texas.
Kuhn's sound is crucial in establishing the awareness of change
and the anticipation of a journey; for example, his recordings of
a stirring wind exert a powerful impact on the imagination.
Walking through the entrance, moving further away from the
everyday world and closer into Wilson's vision, one encounters
additional sounds, including the bird calls made by actress
Jutta Lampe in Wilson's *Orlando*. The walls are covered with
enlargements of Wilson's photographs of tree bark (made for
use as projected images in *The Forest*, but omitted in the
finished piece). On top of the bark abstractions hang a group of
Wilson's photographs of time-worn portraits sculpted in stone.
Each photograph has a frame of mirrored glass that reflects the
viewer's face at the moment of beginning the voyage.

ROOM I

I once had a house in Texas. A small house with a garden, and I had filled it with beautiful things – furniture, carpets, drawings, silver, glass, flowers. I really loved this house; I felt at ease there. Then I went to New York for a few years to work and left it to Bob Wilson, with all the beautiful things it contained. A few months later I came back to spend a few days with Bob in the little house. I didn't recognize it. Everything was still there, but everything had been changed. Repainted, redone, rearranged. There were colors everywhere I couldn't even name; objects had been placed next to one another in what to me was a senseless arrangement; other things had been dragged in, weird stuff – rocks, cacti, enormous pieces of wood, strange fabrics. I didn't feel easy there any more. It all made me anxious, it all seemed odd. But after a few days, little by little, slowly, I started to feel a pleasure that charmed me more and more. For I began looking at the things that surrounded me. Bob knew, by some art, how to arrange them in a way that made me look at them, and to look at them as themselves. I realized that I had previously arranged everything in the house as a frame for myself; I had confined the things in it to a background. Bob had brought things out into the world – or rather he knew how to create a world of mutual affinities between us and objects. He surrounded them in a light which made me see, as if for the first time, those things I had lived with for so long. I kept looking at them. And it seemed to me that they were looking back, and smiling.[3]

Paul Schmidt

Beyond the forest prologue with its enveloping canopy is an expansive, light-filled room where objects and creatures have the freedom to float and fly, to be larger or smaller than normal. The aesthetic intent of this room is to materialize those clear, heightened visualizations that we experienced in childhood and might fleetingly recapture in dreams and hallucinations. The whiteness of this room, the use of natural light, and the way in which the objects so fully inhabit the space (hanging from the ceiling, and either hugging or towering above the floor) create a feeling of boundless possibility. Wilson makes ordinary things shrink or loom large in the convincingly irrational

manner of the surreal or the Alice-in-Wonderland fantastic. His architectural and decorative understanding of scale, proportion, and light, and his keen ability to orchestrate them in a given space help Wilson to realize these fantasies.

By maintaining the vision of an innocent, and practicing a bold transparency of means and materials, Wilson articulates the inner character of his objects. The light and empty bamboo frame of the large *Knee Plays Bird* enhances one's imagining of it soaring in flight, just as the black silk of the *Panther Costume* evokes the sleek majesty of the beast. The most representational and accurately scaled human form in the room is that of a golem, the creature of Jewish folklore, assembled like a robot and given life to help its creators. The *Golem Costume*, worn by an actor in *Death Destruction and Detroit II*, is a hat, mask, and long overcoat modeled in papier mache made from Asian newspapers. The character appeared on stage encased in the costume's armorlike parts, which are tied together with laces. A man in rabbi's black hat and white apron cut open the lacings and revealed the actor inside wearing the same (but now real) hat and overcoat. The golem's first movements were guided by human manipulators with sticks (as in Japanese Bunraku theater), showing him to be an automaton. Wilson conceived this artificial man as something quite literally molded to a human form. With the same forthrightness with which his bird and panther evoke natural freedoms, his golem suggests the constraints of civilization.

The presence of a somber, isolated earth-bound golem in this airy room of light and imagination establishes the note of contradiction essential to Wilson. "It is dangerous to believe in one thing too much. Contradictions are necessary," he stated in 1987.[4] Thus, this project which he calls *The Night before The Day* begins in brightness and proceeds towards night. Some of Wilson's single objects express his involvement with ambiguity and paradox. His metal meshwork sculptures of furniture forms are suspended by thin wires from the ceiling. The sculptures are positioned and lit with a single light source in order to cast a precise shadow on the wall behind them: the silhouette of the shadow might seem almost as substantial as the object itself, and thereby introduce a system of oppositions between form and shadow, reality and illusion, and the various meanings of

Preceding pages:
Tree bark photographs, 1988
Photos by Robert Wilson.

40

light and darkness. In *The Life and Times of Sigmund Freud* (1969) Wilson used the slow descent of a suspended chair as one of the ways to measure and distinguish the acts, and to suggest his process of bringing a picture slowly into focus: in the first act, set on an empty beach, it hung one third of the distance from the top of the proscenium arch to the stage; by the third and last act it had reached the floor and stood beside a table inside a cave.

At first glance, the *Einstein Chair* is a graceful, even serene, object. Its tall thin silhouette, rising from a low square base, and its industrial finish might echo our extended awareness of time and space since Albert Einstein developed his theory of relativity. Other aspects of this sculpture–some sinister, some humble and humorous–become apparent with closer inspection, and with knowledge of both Einstein and Wilson. The sculpture is an elaboration of the chair used as the witness stand in the courtroom scene of *Einstein on the Beach*. The original prop had a stretcher that allowed the actor to mount its wooden seat before testifying. For the sculpture, Wilson exaggerated the design to the point of nonfunction, and created an aesthetic statement of Giacometti-esque hyperattenuation. Viewed as a skeletal, existentialist expression of vulnerability before the law, it suggests the trial Einstein might have inflicted on himself for his contributions to the nuclear age. On the other hand, its materials – galvanized pipes and joints – evoke Einstein's childlike qualities, and allude to his remark in 1954 that if he were a young man again he would consider becoming a plumber rather than a scientist.

Wilson's theater often incorporates patterned sequences of silence and slowness (corollary expressions of abstract space) to open up the viewer's perceptions and thoughts. Generally restrained in form, color, and stance, many of the objects in Room I exemplify his understanding of quiet, spareness, and harmony. He has studied various cultural celebrations of simplicity, whether the most refined statements of the Japanese, the ancient Greeks, the neoclassicists, and the modernists, or those vernacular expressions that achieve great simplicity, such as the artifacts of the American Shaker sect. This perspective was useful in the invention of the *Knee Plays Puppet*, a human protagonist of all times and places, which was

created for the entr'actes of the multinational production the *CIVIL warS*. The puppet, while given male shoulders and hips, was animated by both male and female dancers wearing similar white laboratory uniforms. Its gold face recalls various ancient cultures, from Egypt to Mexico, although the minimal, geometricized face seems closest to those of the Neolithic idols found on the Cycladic Islands. The black linen rectangular torso has a Japanese aspect, and its undecorated jointed limbs, while standard puppet features, recall Oskar Schlemmer's geometricization of the body in his Bauhaus theater pieces and designs of the 1920s.

The familiar, non-threatening sound elements that Hans Peter Kuhn brings together in the sound environment for Room I challenge ordinary perceptions of space. Like the Wilson objects they complement, the sounds address a fluid awareness rather than one that is contained and unified: in this context, the familiar can become strange and suggestive. For example, the sound of water in the kitchen sink overlays resonant tapping noises, which might in this context seem extraterrestrial, but are in fact the sounds made by workers hammering paving stones in Berlin. Eight speakers, each presenting a different sound at moderate volume, are evenly distributed in the corners and sides of the room. The combination of sounds varies with one's position in the room, and each sound evokes space strongly and clearly, creating an unusually sculptural quality.

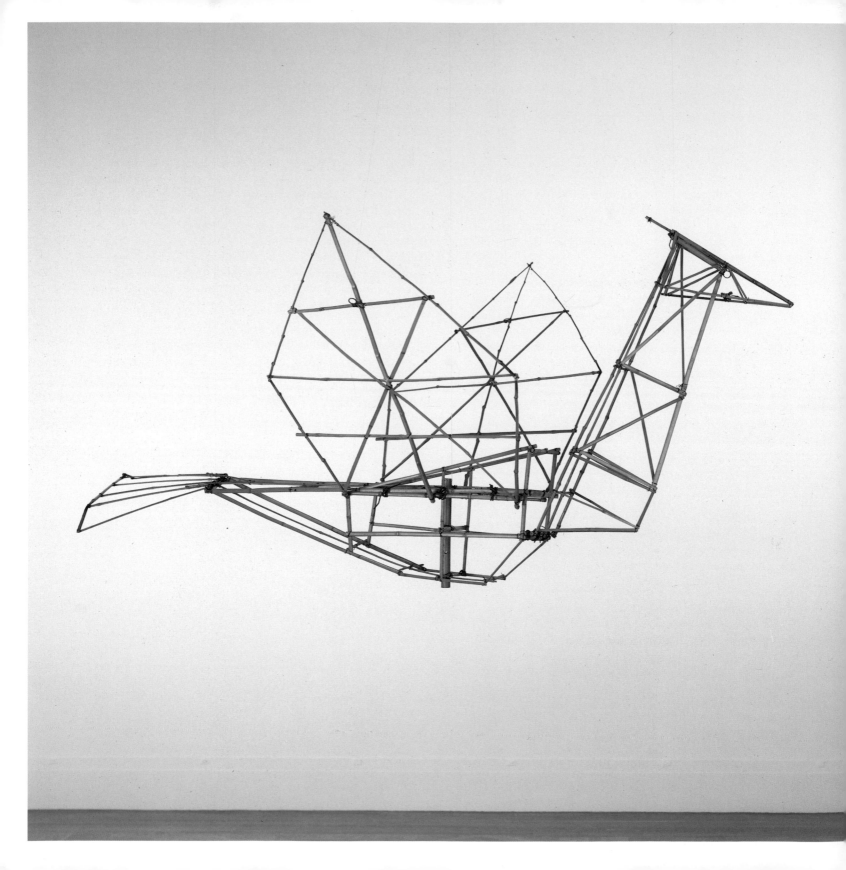

Bird in performance of *The Knee Plays* from *the CIVIL warS,*
Walker Arts Center, Minneapolis, 1984
Photo by Jo Ann Verburg.

Facing page:
Bird (The Knee Plays from *the CIVIL warS),* 1984
Approx. 39 x 100 x 91 in.
Byrd Hoffman Foundation, Inc. Photo by Museum of Fine Arts, Boston

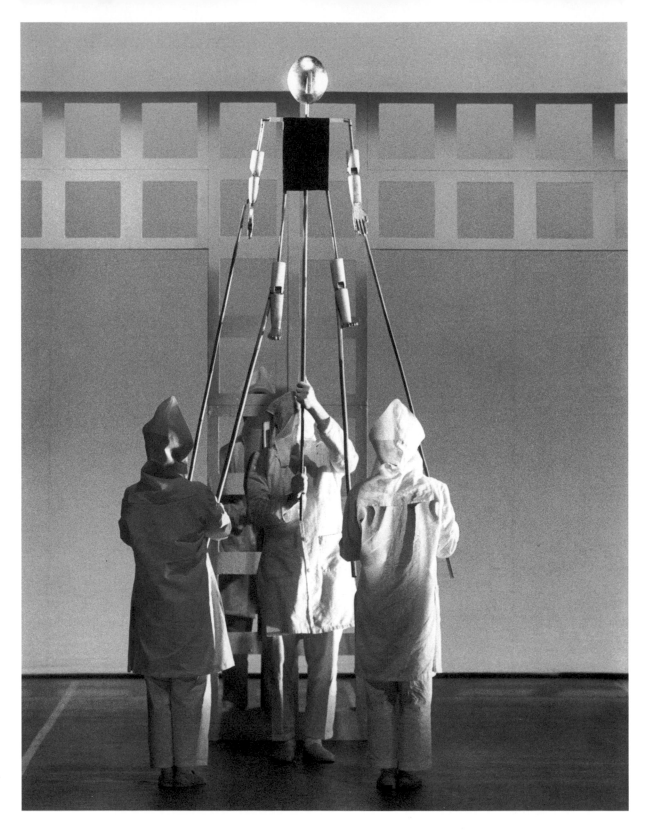

Knee Plays Puppet in performance of *The Knee Plays* from *the CIVIL warS,* Theater der Welt, 1985. Photos by Friedmann Simon

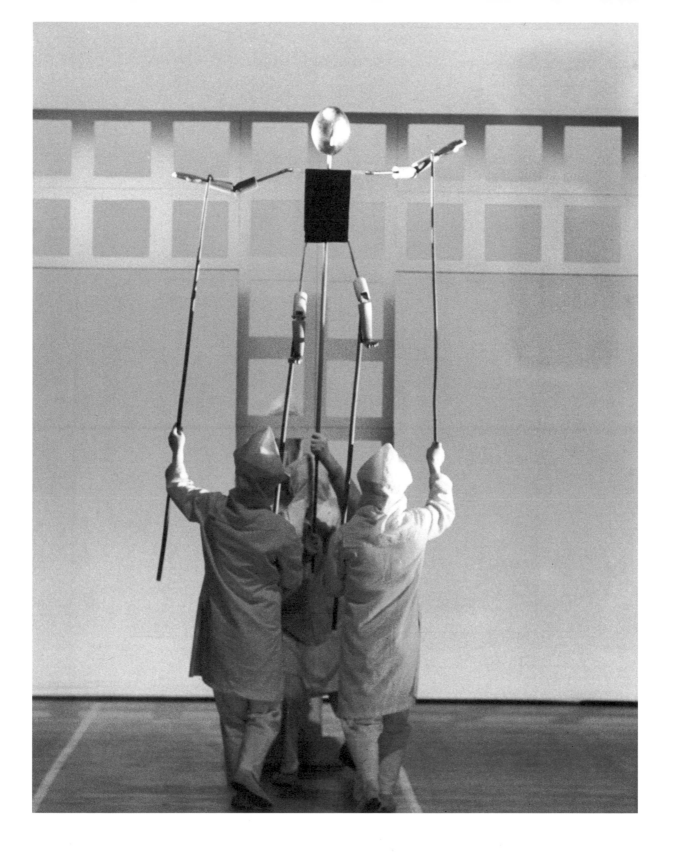

Panther Costume in performance of *Death Destruction and Detroit II,* Schaubühne Theater, Berlin, 1987
Photo by Ruth Walz.

Facing page:
Panther Costume, 1987
12 x 12 x 132 in.
Byrd Hoffman Foundation, Inc. Photo by Museum of Fine Arts, Boston.

Light Bulb in performance of *Death Destruction and Detroit I*,
Schaubühne Theater, Berlin, 1979.

Photo by Ruth Walz.

Facing page:
Light Bulb, 1979
34 x 17 x 17 in.
Byrd Hoffman Foundation, Inc. Photo by Museum of Fine Arts, Boston.

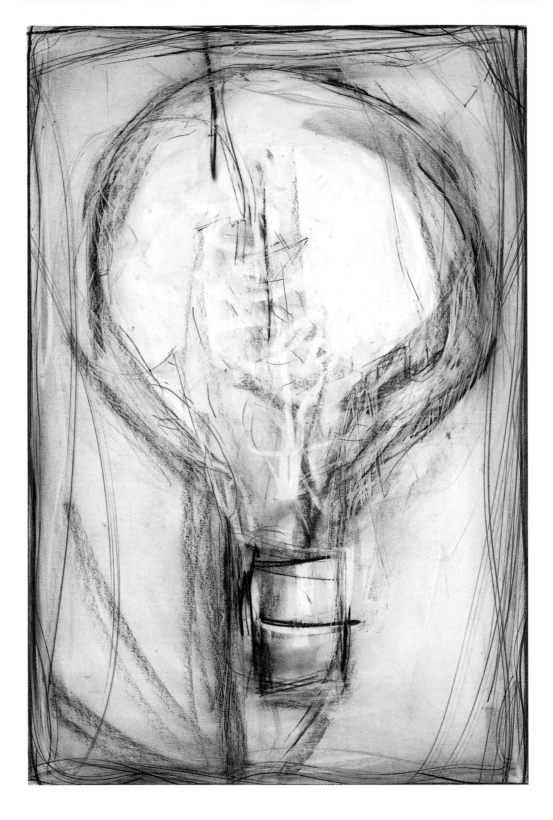

Death Destruction and Detroit I, 1989. Drawing, 43 x 28¾ in.

Breakfast Chairs (Cosmopolitan Greetings), 1988
39⅓ x 17¾ x 17¾ in.
Editions Dosi Delfini/RW Work Ltd. Paula Cooper Gallery. Photo by Best Fotografie.

Hanging Table (The Life and Times of Sigmund Freud), 1969. 23½ x 5½ x 34½ in.

Robert Wilson. Photo by Museum of Fine Arts, Boston.

Hanging Chair (The Life and Times of Sigmund Freud), 1969. 35½ x 9½ x 9½ in.
Robert Wilson. Photo by Museum of Fine Arts, Boston.

Performances of *Einstein on the Beach,* 1976
Byrd Hoffman Foundation, Inc. Photos by Fulvio Roiter.

Facing page:
Einstein Chair (left), 1976 design,
1985 edition, 89⅛ x 9⅞ in.
Museum of Fine Arts, Boston.

Little Chair (right), 1985, 15⅞ x 4⅝ x 5½ in.
Robert Wilson. Photo by Museum of Fine Arts, Boston.

Prototype for *Parzival: a Chair with a Shadow*, 1987
41¾ x 15 x 15¾ in.

Thomas Ammann. Photo courtesy of Byrd Hoffman Foundation, Inc.

Facing page:
Jutta Lampe with *Little Door* in performance of *Orlando*,
Schaubühne Theater, Berlin, 1989

Photo by Ruth Walz.

Little Door (Orlando), 1989
11 x 7⅝ x 2⅓ in.

Annemarie Verna Galerie, Zürich. Photo by Thomas Cugini.

Golem Suit in performance of *Death Destruction and Detroit II*, Schaubühne Theater, Berlin, 1987. Photo by Ruth Walz.

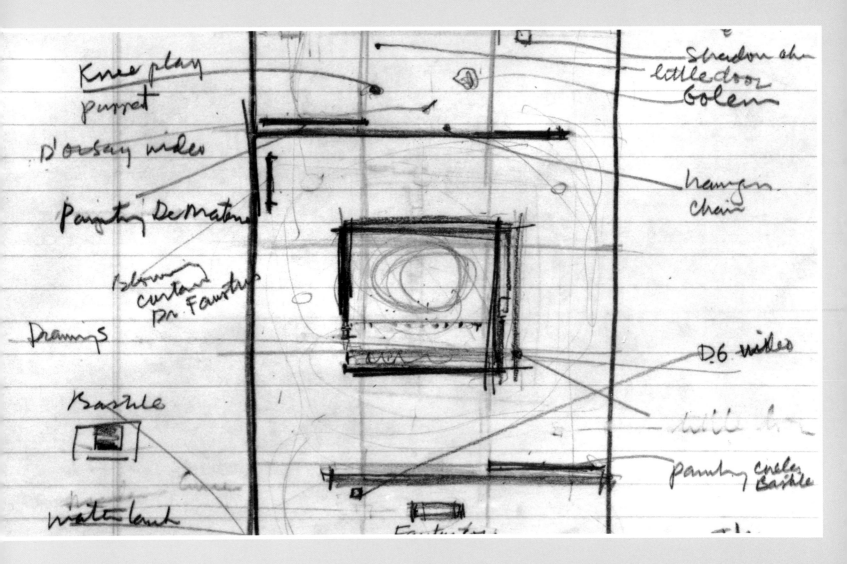

Detail of plan for the installation of "Robert Wilson's Vision," 1989.

ROOM II

There is no such thing as ultimate forgetting; traces once impressed upon the memory are indestructible; a thousand accidents may interpose a veil between our present consciousness and the secret inscriptions of the mind. Accidents of the same sort will also rend away this veil. But alike, whether veiled or unveiled, the inscription remains forever; just as stars seem to withdraw before the common light of day, whereas in fact, we all know that it is the light which is drawn over them as a veil; and they are waiting to be revealed, whenever the obscuring daylight itself shall have withdrawn.[5]
Thomas De Quincey

The dense hanging of framed drawings in Room II might suggest the stones and blocks of a massive foundation. The ordered claustrophobia of the perimeter walls is heightened by the large structure at the center of the room. Illuminated models of Wilson's theater sets are embedded in one of its outer surfaces. Walking around this blocky structure, the viewer finds a corner doorway to its interior. Inside is a new version of Wilson's 1987 tableau *Memory of a Revolution*, originally made for the Galerie der Stadt, Stuttgart, in response to an invitation to create a work about Napoleon.

Inside the installation gilded and upholstered chairs, such as might be found in the royal box of a European theater, are lined up with their backs against the wall. An iron grille separates the chairs from a rat-infested prison cell. A colossal elephant leg thrusts down in the midst of the rats. A tiny stone-walled room has been carved into the elephant foot, and an old man in late-eighteenth-century costume sits inside it, holding on his lap a model of a theater interior. Beneath the model's proscenium arch a red-dressed diva stands at stage center; Maria Callas is heard singing arias from Luigi Cherubini's opera *Medea,* which was written in Paris and first performed there in 1797.

The installation addresses the history of the site where the Bastille, an enormous fourteenth-century fortress and prison, once stood. In 1789 revolutionaries ransacked this symbol of oppression, whose parapets had become a favorite site for aristocratic diversions; only sixteen people were found inside

its prison quarters. The story can be continued in the words of art historian Robert Rosenblum: "Of these Napoleonic resurrections of imperial splendor, the most unusual was [the] huge plaster elephant at the Place de la Bastille… For Napoleon, the elephant [erected in 1814] was a symbol of Caesar and of the Emperor, and as such, it contributed as fully as the Roman temples, triumphal arches, and victory columns to the imperialization of Paris. Later in the nineteenth century, under radically changing social conditions … the elephant of the Bastille was to be commemorated by Victor Hugo in *Les Misérables* (1862) as the pitiful dwelling place of the Parisian street urchin, Gavroche. Indeed, after the fall of Napoleon, the capacity of Greco-Roman antiquity to be revitalized in France for political ends was lost; and the classical world was transformed, instead, into a hermetically sealed domain, inhabited by aesthetes and archeologists who either ignored or opposed the profound new challenges of nineteenth-century experience."[6] Napoleon intended that the three-story-high plaster elephant would be replaced by a bronze one whose trunk functioned as the spout of a fountain, but this never happened. After Napoleon's demise the restored Bourbon Monarchy employed an old Bonapartist to reside in one of the elephant legs and act as caretaker of the plaster monument. Gradually it fell into disrepair, and was overrun with rats (a nightmarish scenario graphically described in Victor Hugo's novel). It was torn down in 1846, and never replaced.

In 1987, when Wilson made *Memory of a Revolution*, French government plans were well underway for the creation of another monument at the Place de la Bastille. A new opera house was being built to open on the bicentennial of the revolution (July 14, 1989), and Wilson had been engaged as an artistic director of the inaugural concert. Thus the old man in the prison cell of the installation–whether prisoner or watchman– holds the seed of the future opera house.

Memory of a Revolution demonstrates Wilson's sophisticated approach to history, his involvement with the continuum of space and time, and his concern for the relationship of the fragment and the whole within that continuum. He fosters new relationships, insights, and meanings by layering and juxtaposing materials without obvious or logical connections. It should hardly be surprising, then, that a favorite metaphor of

Wilson's in the early 1970s was the onion. In one of the hundreds of scenes at the seven-day performance he staged in Iran in 1972, Sheryl Sutton sat completely still, and used the smallest possible amount of energy to peel away the layers of a single onion. It was over two hours before the onion's center finally disappeared. In such a time frame the action transcends the tears and smells associated with the onion and becomes a metaphor for an infinity of interconnections; the static performer assumes the stature of a cosmic creator or prophet.

Like one of the layers of an onion, Wilson's drawings are integral to, yet to some extent independent of, the larger body of his work. Some are informal studies or notations for the staging or lighting of his theater: he produces countless scribbles, sketches, and diagrams over dinner and in meetings. His more formal, more finished, and more interpretive drawings, are featured in Room II. This type is often made in the months during which a new work is being planned and rehearsed, but Wilson may also make a drawing as an opportunity to return to a scene after the production has closed. These finished drawings have been a source of income (when, for example, raising funds for *the CIVIL warS*). In recent years he routinely chooses a suite of the best of these for a gallery exhibition scheduled to coincide with the new production. In 1989, working with a professional scene painter, he made a large painting based on a finished drawing, and he proposes to continue producing these large stretched canvases.

The dense clustering of drawings in Room II parallels Wilson's theatrical collaging or layering of independent parts. Describing the way in which he wants text to be encountered in his theater he has said: "I try not to illustrate the text directly, but to set up a space in which we can hear it [and] think about it."[7] Similarly his drawings suggest so many thoughts culled from his active imagination. They fall into three loosely defined periods: the youthful experimentalism of the earliest works; the development of story-board sequencing and schematized imagery in the mid-1970s; and the elaboration of a more nuanced, more painterly grand manner in the 1980s. (Wilson was awarded the Skowhegan Medal for Drawing in 1987.) The drawings record a contest between the light of the paper and the dark of the markings, as Wilson struggles to capture the flash of the imagination. He usually puts down masking tape to define the edges that will contain his image on the sheet of paper. The lightest smearing or rubbing of graphite gives a mist or thin shadow; a barrage of aggressive strokes ruptures the paper surface on occasion; an intense build-up of graphite sometimes gives the paper the sheen of metal; deft eraser strokes capture flashes of light in motion. When the masking tape is removed, a sharp edge demarcates the arena of markings and gestures. The gesturalism of Wilson's working method echoes his interest to Action Painting during his years as a student.

Wilson has developed his own vocabulary of forms in his drawings. The block, the cube, the shaft, the pyramid, and the curtain of light appear either as solids, or, more frequently, as bodies of light defining the darkness. These forms recur in endless variations of scale, mood, and subject, communicating the monolithic solidity of a wall, a room, or a building; the punctuation of space by tree trunks, columns, or giant figures; or the openness of a lake, a desert, a sky, or a window. The unity of form and content that underlies many of the drawings is comparable to Wilson's practice of reworking and transforming scenes from earlier theater works into new statements. Thus the colossal elephant leg in *Memory of a Revolution* (1987) echoes the giant cat legs that crossed the stage in *The King of Spain* (1969); furthermore the immense tree trunk that descends into an empty stage in *Orlando* (1989) may derive, unconsciously at least, from the elephant leg.

The speakers between the outer walls and the small room containing *Memory of a Revolution* play Hans Peter Kuhn's 1989 harpsichord compositions for Wilson's *Orlando*. While the historicism of its baroque style emphasizes the anachronistic salon-like hanging of the drawings, the music has been processed through a computer so that each note comes from a different speaker. This effect warps the genteel associations of the music, and reinforces the subtle dizziness induced by dozens of images, which seem to saturate the room.

Four drawings for *Cosmopolitan Greetings*, 1988
Each sheet 17¾ x 24 in.

Installation photographs of *Memory of a Revolution*, 1987
Courtesy of Staatsgalerie, Stuttgart.

Medea (Act III)
Drawing, 2¾ x 29 in.
Paula Cooper Gallery, New York. Photo by Museum of Fine Arts, Boston.

Model for the set of *the CIVIL warS* (Act 1, scene C), 1984.
Fabricated by Tom Kamm

Byrd Hoffman Foundation, Inc. Photo by Museum of Fine Arts, Boston.

Facing page:
the CIVIL warS, 1983
Vertical scroll, 147½ x 54 in.

Paula Cooper Gallery, New York. Photo by Museum of Fine Arts, Boston.

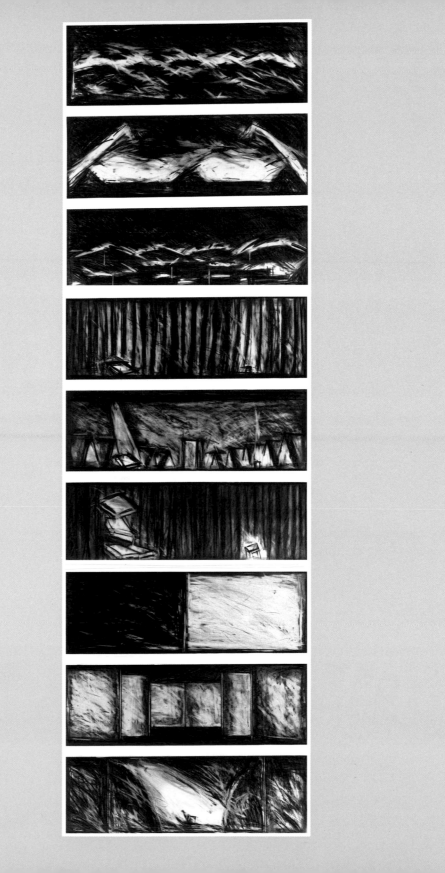

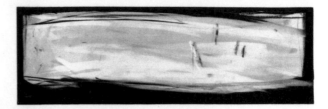
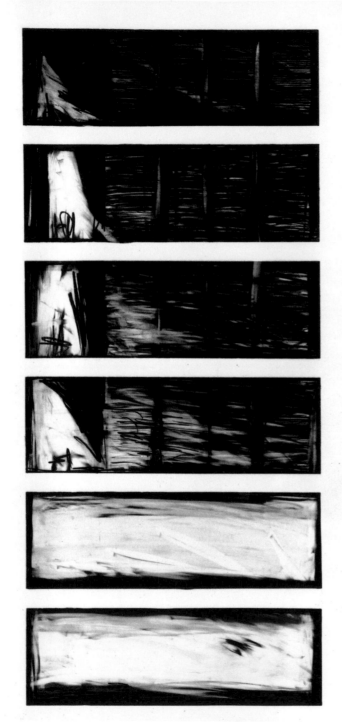

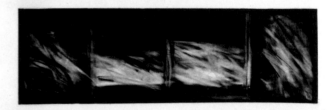

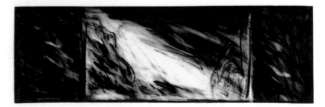

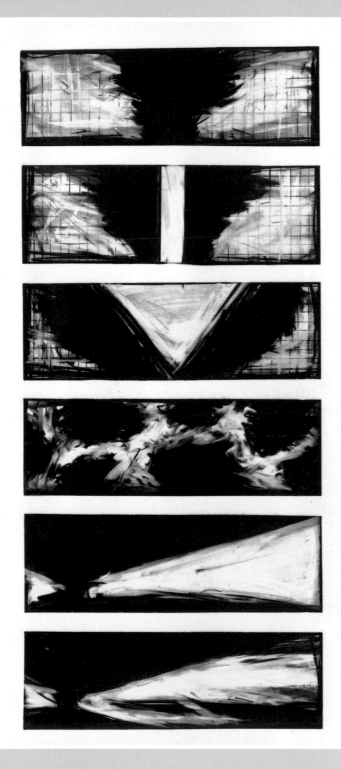

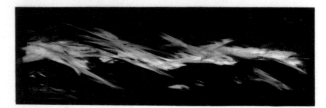

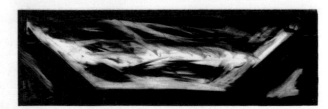

Following pages (75–79):
the CIVIL warS, 1983
Horizontal storyboard, 54 x 235½ in.
Paula Cooper Gallery, New York. Photo by Museum of Fine Arts, Boston.

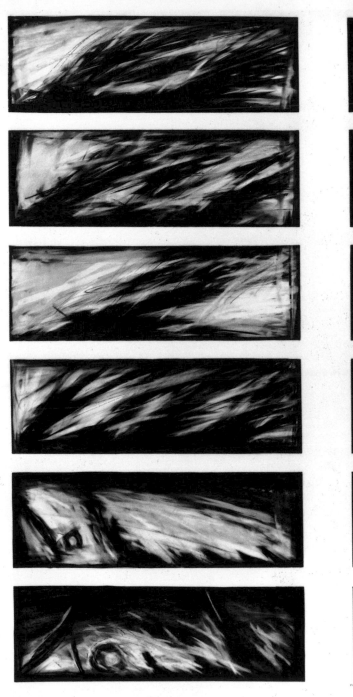
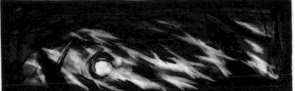

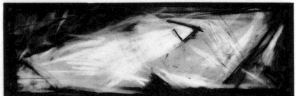

"THE CIVIL WARS: a tree is best measured when it is down"

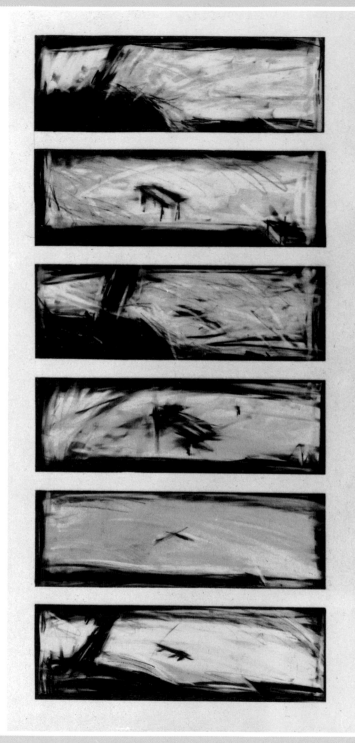
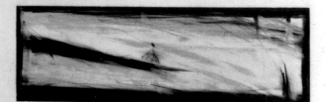
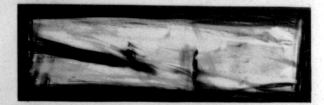

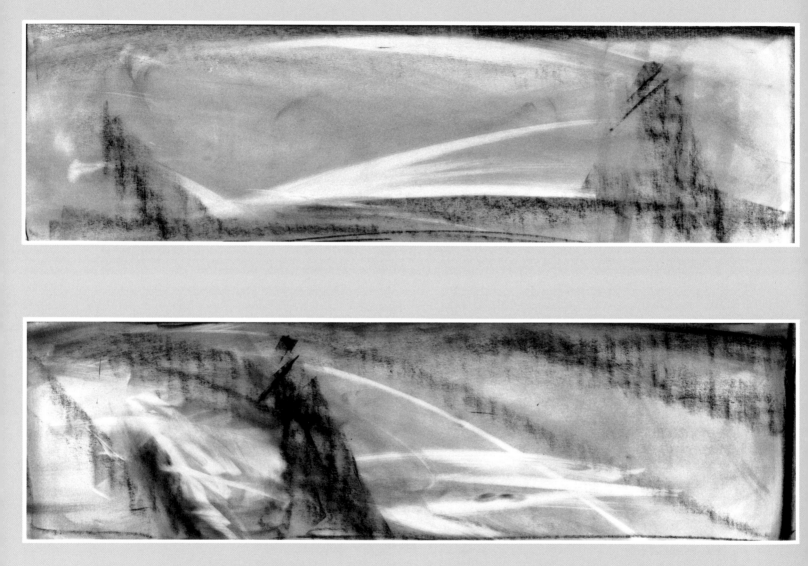

Four drawings for *the CIVIL warS* (Act 1, scene B), 1982
Each sheet 7½ x 26 in.

Asher Edelman, New York. Photo by Museum of Fine Arts, Boston.

Doktor Faustus (Act 1, Blowing Curtain)
Drawing, 24⅝ x 37⅞ in.

Paula Cooper Gallery, New York. Photo by James Dee.

Parsifal (Act II), 1985
Drawing, 27⅝ x 39⅛ in.

Paula Cooper Gallery, New York. Photo by Geoffrey Clements.

Model for set of *Swan Song*, 1989. Fabricated by Vera Dobroschke. Byrd Hoffman Foundation, Inc. Photo by Museum of Fine Arts, Boston.

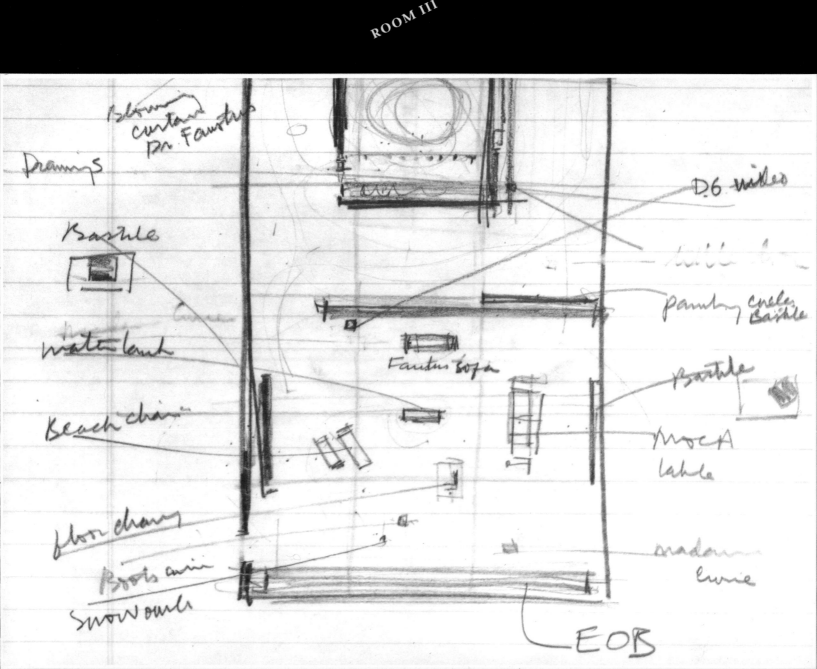

ROOM III

Forest

It is a place of verdure, of fresh green; of wind – windy places, in wind, windy; a place of cold: it becomes cold; there is much frost; it is a place which freezes. It is a place from which misery comes, where it exists; a place where there is affliction – a place of affliction, of lamentation, a place of affliction, of weeping; a place where there is sadness, a place of compassion, of sighing; a place which arouses sorrow, which spreads misery... There is fright, there is constant fright. One is devoured; one is slain by stealth; one is abused; one is brutally put to death; one is tormented. Misery abounds. There is calm, constant calm, continuing calm.[8]

Aztec definition

This quotation presents the forest as a setting inimical to Aztec culture. It would not have served to introduce the discussion of the enchanting forest-like entrance section of *The Night before The Day*. However, in 1987 Wilson used this poetic Aztec description to great effect in the theater. The text was read in a quiet manner in the second act of *Death Destruction and Detroit II* during two consecutive scenes filled with images that elicited yearning and vulnerability, and the fear these states can engender. "In the Sky" (scene 12) was wistful and lonely, and accompanied by sad string music: the black shoes and trouser cuffs of a giant man passed slowly across one of the four stages Wilson created; elsewhere a magic carpet flew through the sky, and on a high pedestal a woman in a red dress burned letters with the authority of a sibyl. In "Thunderstorm" (scene 13) a frail old man tottered across a vast landscape; as he passed the little piles of sticks lining his path, flashes of lightning burned them up. The barely suppressed anguish within these two scenes from the theater is now recalled by Wilson in Room III of *The Night before The Day*.

The dark spirit in the third and last large room contrasts to the bright innocence of the first. The technological aura of urban culture replaces the natural wonderment of Room I. As evoked by Wilson and Kuhn, technology has frightening and dehumanizing guises that compete with its thrilling and optimistic power. The lighting in this space is artificial; spotlights and other special effects make this most conspicuous. Covering the wall facing the entrance is the modular structure of flashing control panels from the spaceship interior of *Einstein on the Beach*. Each unit (almost seven feet square) has a backboard studded with small light bulbs flashing in programmed patterns. The light panels are incorporated into a scaffold of metal pipes with catwalks. The horizontal, vertical, diagonal, and circular patterns generated on the grid of lightbulbs are based on a diagram of dance movements created by Lucinda Childs for the first production of *Einstein*. Two small elevators, one moving vertically, the other horizontally, slowly travel back and forth in front of the scaffold. The elevator that moves vertically carries a clock that runs backwards and the horizontal elevator carries a compass; for Wilson they symbolized time and space, respectively. The light panels flash quickly changing patterns until a certain moment in their cycle when most of the lights in Room III dim. Suddenly, loud mechanical noises drown out the other elements of the sound environment and a spotlight reveals a small rocket that ascends diagonally across the room until it reaches the ceiling. When its journey is complete, the lights of the wall panels begin to flash again, and the sounds return. Thus, light and sound effects alternate, first giving the visitor the sense of being in the brightly lit control room of the spaceship, and then of watching its journey through darkness.

The furniture sculptures in this room are strident and imposing. The two aggressively shiny and angular *Beach Chairs* from *Death Destruction and Detroit* challenge the standard connotations of relaxation at the beach: their uninviting forms provide an Orwellian vision of what could happen when the mechanistic obsessions of industrialized society are ruthlessly applied to the accoutrements of leisure. Beauty in such an extreme situation becomes hard, implacable, and evil. The long, rectilinear, red lacquer sofa, presented in a red spotlight, is based on the whore's sofa in Wilson's 1989 *Doktor Faustus*. The sounds brought together by Hans Peter Kuhn affirm incipient unease: a voice is heard yelling across a great distance; a telephone rings incessantly; a dog barks. The crash of cymbals is stretched out and manipulated into an "abstract" sound. This undercurrent of angst is related to the difficult aspects of

Wilson's theater: the moments of discord between what is heard, for example, and what is observed; the sense of understanding less and less what is going on, and an awareness of logic and meaning being abandoned; the obsessive repetition of distressing images, words or screams; the slow pacing or endless wait for change or resolution. Wilson's theater moves forward by balancing such sharp discord with more pleasant illusions, tempering the imaginary with the real. Similarly Rooms I and III hinge and balance upon Room II. However, within Room III the throbbing lights and harnessed power of technology are tempered by a sense of melancholy about the history and predicament of the earth. One response is to long for a return to the beginning of the exhibition. Such a desire need not involve flight either to the past or to innocence. It can confirm that life's journey is not just a simple passage from light to dark, but a layering of such cycles and patterns of experience.

Room III is not unremittingly bleak. Knowledge, experience, and warmth intervene to lighten it with humanity. Critics sometimes overlook, or dismiss as naive, Wilson's broad humor and his gentle optimism. Depending on the viewer's attitude to American Wild West culture, Wilson's casts of two cowboy boots, standing alone in a spotlight in the center of Room III, may evoke good, bad, or indifferent thoughts about the maverick mentality; they also have a capacity to delight with their funky and ridiculous improbability. Wilson's guarded optimism is evident in the epilogue of *Einstein on the Beach*. Following immediately after the mounting sense of chaos and nuclear apocalypse experienced during the opera's final act (set in the spaceship interior) the conclusion presents two silent lovers sitting in the moonlight on a park bench in the middle of nowhere. A bus approaches slowly. The bus driver's text (written by Samuel M. Johnson, the African-American actor who was seventy-seven years old when he first performed the role) begins as follows: "The day with all its cares and perplexities is ended and the night is now upon us. The night should be a time of peace and tranquility, a time to relax and be calm. We have need of a soothing story to banish disturbing thoughts of the day, to set at rest our troubled minds, and put at ease our ruffled spirits. And what sort of story shall we hear? Ah, it will

be a familiar story, a story that is so very, very old, and yet it is so new. It is the old, old story of love." Here again is the contradiction Wilson embraces. In *The Night before The Day* the nightlike last room houses irrational and nightmarish visions in the spirit of Goya, while at the close of *Einstein* night occasions post-apocalyptic peace and liberation.

Beach Chairs (Death Destruction and Detroit), 1979
31 x 78½ x 23¾ and 22 x 78½ x 23¾ in.

Walker Art Center, Minneapolis.

Esmeralda's Bed, 1989
81⅞ x 18½ x 36¼ in.
Paula Cooper Gallery. Photo courtesy of Byrd Hoffman Foundation, Inc.

I was sitting on my patio this guy appeared I thought I was hallucinating, 1977
Drawing, 21¾ x 29½ in.

Asher Edelman, New York. Photo by Geoffrey Clements.

Facing page:

Chair for Marie Curie (De Materie), 1989
15¾ x 11¾ x 54 in.

RW Work, Ltd. Photo courtesy of Byrd Hoffman Foundation, Inc.

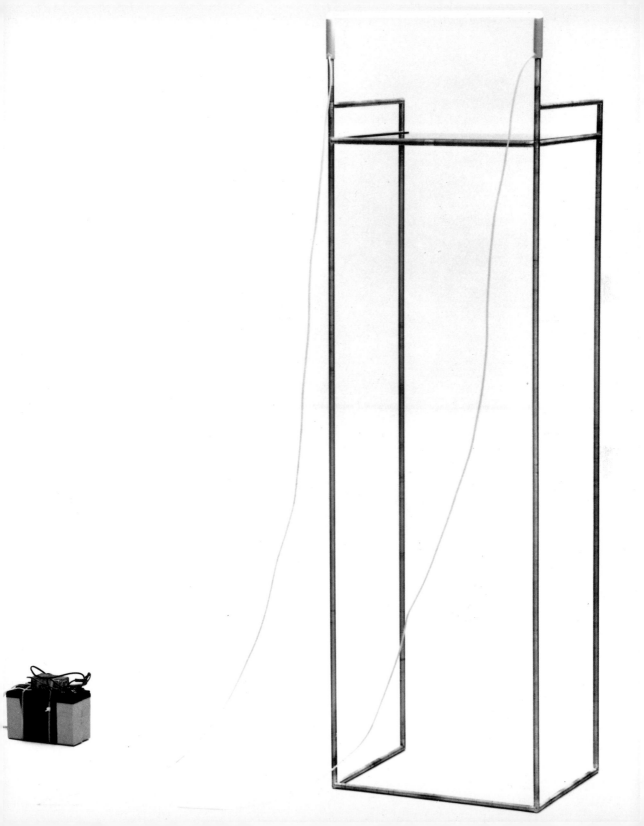

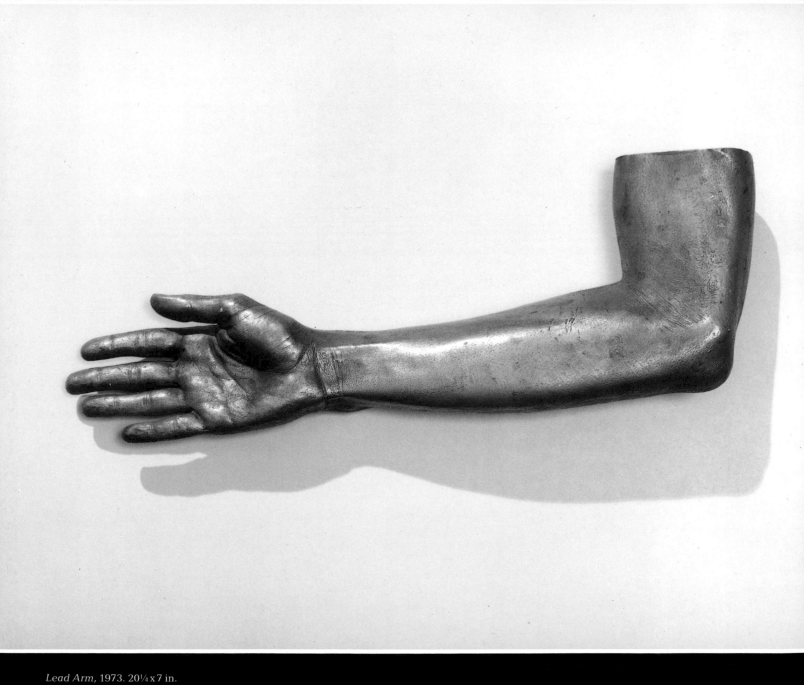

Lead Arm, 1973. 20¼ x 7 in.

Private Collection. Photo by James Dee.

Cowboy Boots, 1973. 13½ x 13 x 4½ in.

Four drawings for *Alceste*, 1986. Each approx. 28½ x 39 in. Paula Cooper Gallery, New York. Photos by Geoffrey Clements.

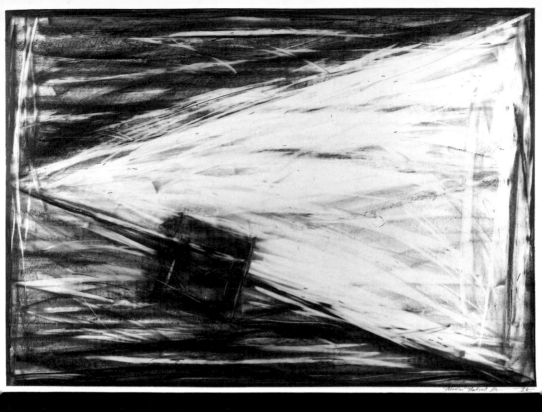

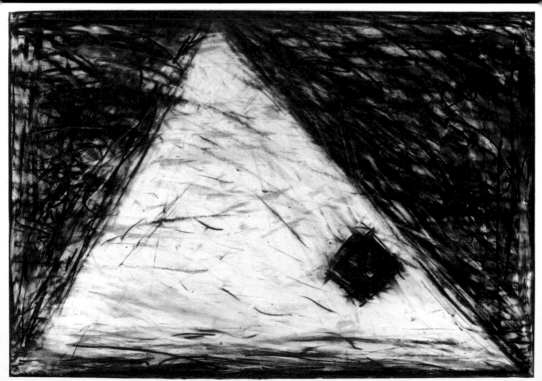

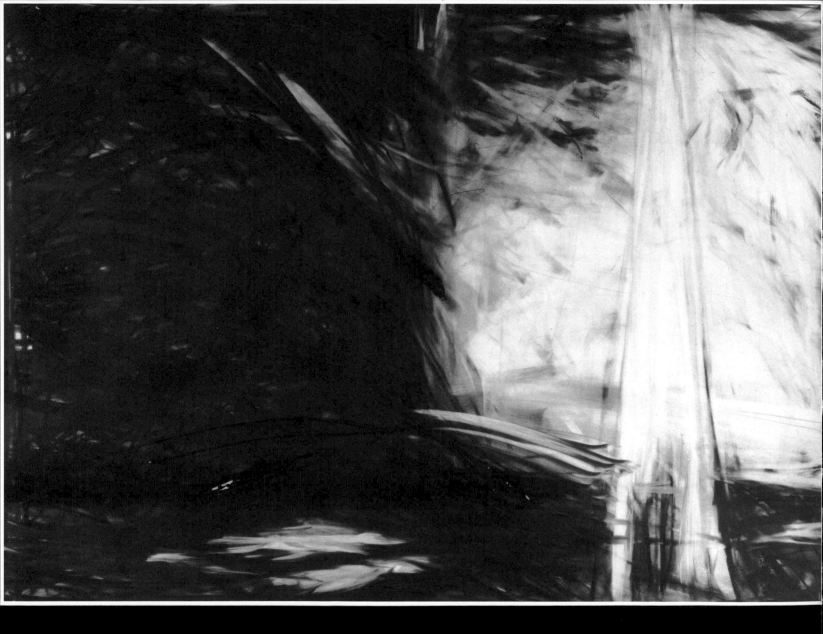

Great Day in the Morning, 1982
Drawing, 23 x 29 in.

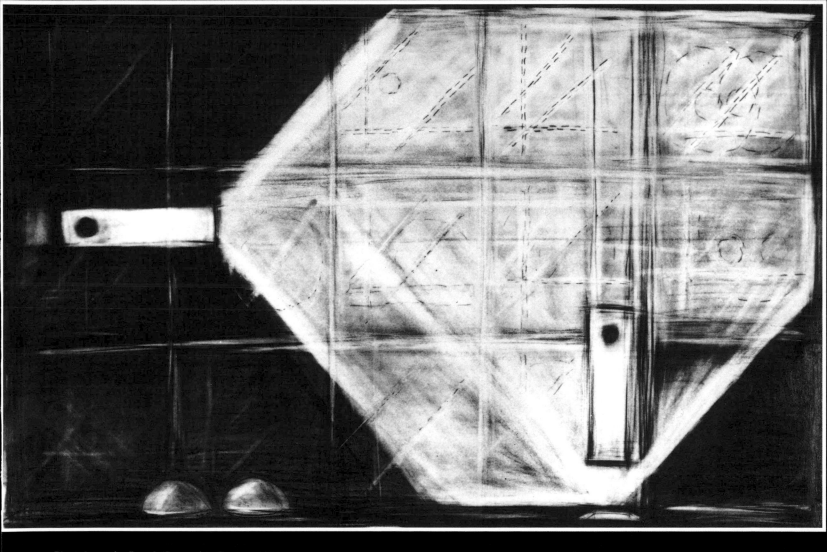

Einstein on the Beach (Spaceship Scene), 1976
Drawing, 25¾ x 39⅝ in.

Performance of *Einstein on the Beach* (Spaceship
Teatro La Fenice, Venice, 1976.
Byrd Hoffman Foundation, Inc. Photo by Fulvio Roiter.

Following page:
Robert Wilson in performance of *Overture to Deaf*
Barcelona, 1986.
Photo by Morera & Morera

EPILOGUE: VIDEO ROOM

It would be [a mistake] to categorise [Wilson's] work as pure formalism. Though often hermetic, and containing no easy slogans, his productions embody in their very shape and method comments on both philosophical and political values. They achieve this by a highly developed use of alienating effects that were the hallmark of Brechtian theatre practice. In particular, Wilson exploits the technique of using each element on the stage to undercut, contradict or comment on the others. Unlike most directors, he is content for these separate expressive elements to remain fragmented. He resists the temptation to synthesis and in this he manifests his critical commentary on our fragmented age. His productions do not, as [Peter] Brook's so often do, end on an evocation of harmony and resolution.[9]

David Bradby and David Williams

Wilson's five video works were originally to have been distributed about the three large rooms according to their character. The two most playful, *Video 50* (1978) and *Stations* (1982) were sited in the first room, while *Deafman Glance* (1981) and the two short 1989 works, *La Femme à la Cafetière* and *The Death of King Lear*, were chosen for the last. *Deafman Glance* is Wilson's most ambiguous and challenging film, with a darkness befitting Room III. It provides a compellingly personal experience, but cannot be decoded into a single meaning. Sheryl Sutton performs the exquisite, excruciatingly slow actions she and Wilson created in 1970: a woman in a high-necked, long-sleeved, trailing black dress stops washing dishes, pours a glass of milk, takes it upstairs to a young boy, and returns to the kitchen; after washing more dishes she takes a knife, returns to the boy's room, and stabs him in the chest (neither shows any emotions, and the camera shows no blood); all these actions are repeated with a different boy.

In a variety of theater performances, Wilson has joined Sutton to enact mirrored versions of this ritual of love and murder. Starting from a pair of identical tables and props at the center of the stage – Wilson in formal black suit and Sutton in the long black dress – they moved in opposite directions to two children

seated at either end of the stage. The children have been played by boys and by girls. In Spain in 1986 Wilson did the piece as a solo performance in blackface and wore a long robe similar to Sherry Sutton's Victorian dress. Whether on videotape or in live performance, the events are alarming, and the slowness of each succeeding event adds to the unfolding menace. Amy Taubin criticized the videotape as misogynist and politically irresponsible for exploiting black women (victims of oppression in contemporary American society) in the enactment of patriarchal society's phobias about "phallic mothers" and African Americans.[10] But other readings can be made by going beneath the surface of the piece from different perspectives. In lectures Wilson suggests that the black-clad figure can just as well be imagined as an angel of death, a priest, or a contemporary Medea. In several interviews he has cited as inspiration the filmed experiments of his friend Daniel Stern, professor of psychology at Columbia University. Wilson told *The New Yorker* in 1971: "[Stern] is working on a study of babies from the time of birth to the age of three weeks, with cameras and stopped-action films. The baby cries, the mother leans down to pick him up. What we see with our eye is the big movement, the mother loving the baby. But you film it, and look at the isolated first frame of the film, and nine times out of ten what you see is the mother *lunging* at the child. So many different things are going on, and the baby is picking them up. I'd like to deal with these things in the theater, if that's possible. In preparing my people, I just work with the body, trying to get them to really connect with the audience."[11] Stern showed that if the act is viewed slowly enough, a mother's caring reaction involves a perceptible moment of fury, which in turn briefly increases the anxiety of the crying baby.

Wilson claims that he has never understood the murder scene from *Deafman Glance*, which may explain why he returns to it as he does. It is the clearest example of an involvement with relativity in his art. He insists that meaning depends on so many factors that its pointless to ascribe a single interpretation – however obvious it might seem – to a given work of art. Things are perceived differently depending upon the time, space, and frame or context in which they are presented. One intention of all Wilson's art is to stretch our awareness of these conditions:

he wants to teach us to listen with our whole bodies, as a deaf person must, and not only with our ears; and to see with a similarly expanded sensibility. Finally it should be remembered that Wilson exercises his sense of relativity when it comes to understanding how he works as an artist: "I like to work intensely and then forget about it. That way I can come back and look at the piece fresh. I make drawings. Usually after a year or two I know if they're any good or whether to throw them away. It's only by living with them that I really know and it's the same with making a work. I like to work very carefully on a piece then put it aside – live with it – then come back and work. That way it becomes etched in my mind and head."[12]

Notes

1. Peter Sellars, "On Opera," *Artforum* 28 (Dec. 1989), pp. 23-24.
2. Clive Barnes, "Must There Be a Story?," *New York Times*, 14 March 1971, p. D5.
3. Paul Schmidt, "Introduction," *Robert Wilson: Dessins et Sculptures*, Paris, Musée Galliera, 1974.
4. Quoted by Roberto Suro in "Wilson's 'Salome' Will Be 'Normal,'" *New York Times*, 10 January 1987.
5. Thomas De Quincey, "The Pains of Opium," from *The Confessions of an English Opium-Eater*, London: John Lane, 1930, pp. 241-42. 1821.
6. Robert Rosenblum, *Transformations in Late Eighteenth Century Art*, Princeton 1967, pp. 133-34.
7. Wilson speaking at the Sixteenth Amherst Colloquium on German Literature, University of Massachusetts at Amherst, April 28, 1988.
8. Documented in the 16th century by Bernardino de Sahagun, *Florentine Codex: General History of the Things of New Spain*, quoted in *Technicians of the Sacred: A Range of Poetries from Africa, Asia, and Oceania*, collected and edited by Jerome Rothenberg. New York, 1968, pp. 23-24.
9. David Bradby and David Williams, *Directors' Theatre*, (London, 1988), p. 225
10. Amy Taubin, "Talking through Customs at the Video Border," *Alive* (Sept. Oct., 1982), p. 32.
11. The Talk of the Town Column, "Non-Verbal," *New Yorker* 47 (March 27, 1971) p. 30.
12. Wilson quoted by Laurence Shyer in "Robert Wilson: Current Projects," *Theater* 14 (Summer/Fall, 1983)986), pp. 95-96.

Facing page and following page:
Stills from video of *Deafman Glance*, 1981.
Byrd Hoffman Foundation.

105

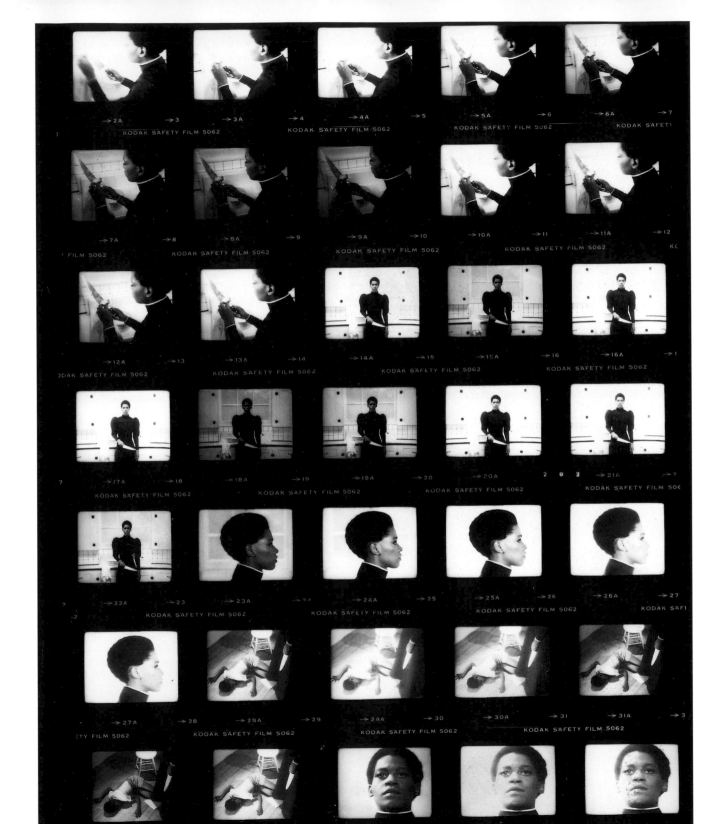

Robert Wilson, 1976
Photo by Robert Mapplethorpe, copyright The Estate of Robert Mapplethorpe.

Robert Wilson, about 1962
Courtesy Byrd Hoffman Foundation.

Poles, Grailville, Ohio, 1968
Courtesy Byrd Hoffman Foundation.

Robert Wilson solo performance, Grailville, Ohio, 1968
Courtesy Byrd Hoffman Foundation.

My introduction to Wilson and his art includes contemporaneous quotations from particularly descriptive or analytical essays and reviews. I have featured them as period contributions rather than paraphrased their insights. This process of assimilation parallels Wilson's method. Restrictions of space make it impossible to acknowledge all performers and technical staff, or to list all of Wilson's lectures, workshop performances, and gallery exhibitions.

1941–58

Born October 4, 1941, Robert Mims Wilson grew up in Waco, Texas, the center of a flat and open region peopled by Baptist farmers. His father, a successful attorney, came from a wealthy background. His mother was raised in an orphanage and worked in an office before marrying. Several nights each week Wilson, his parents, and his younger sister dined formally at home. Wilson remembers his mother seated bolt upright; her silent and emotionless bearing made her hard to approach.

In the second grade a teacher asked Wilson's class what they would like to be when they grew up. Some answered a nurse, a fireman, a house wife. Wilson answered, "The King of Spain." As he later recalled, the teacher said, "'Now *this* child's got problems' and she wrote that on my report card and I remember that my mother kept that card and I remember thinking at that time that it was too bad she didn't see it that way ... In the sixth grade I had won an Art Contest cause I had drawn a magnolia in chalk and it had been placed in the library in a children's Art Show and I had won First Prize and the Waco News Tribune was interviewing me and they said, 'Now tell us, Bob Wilson, What do you think is the Nicest Thing in the Whole World?' And I said a big thick cat paw!! ... I've always been awkward and self-conscious."[1]

Throughout childhood Wilson had a speech impediment that made him take a long time to get words out. Nonetheless, in his early teens he attended the Saturday-afternoon Children's Theater Program at Baylor University. When he was seventeen, he overcame his speech impediment with the help of Miss Byrd Hoffman. She was a dance instructor in her seventies who also worked with brain-damaged children. Wilson took classes with her for several months: "[She] talked to me about the energy in my body, about relaxing, letting energy flow through ... she

would play piano and I would move my body. She didn't watch ... she never taught a technique, she never gave me a way to approach it, it was more that I discovered it on my own."[2] Her example was important to him in later years when he developed his own work as an artist.

At Waco High School, Wilson submitted a non-verbal piece to a drama competition. Years later he remembered it as follows: "Two people in white sat in a room. Now and then there would be a knock on the door. One of them would get up and open it, but there was nobody there. That was all. It became a key piece; I keep going back to it."[3]

1959–62

Wilson attempted to please his father by majoring in business administration at the University of Texas (Austin). During this period he helped with and appeared in Children's Theater productions in Waco and worked with brain-damaged children for the first time. In 1961 some of his paintings were exhibited in a gallery in Dallas. Early in 1962 he dropped out of college to pursue an arts career, and moved to New York City in the fall.

1963

Wilson enrolled in the department of interior design at Pratt Institute, Brooklyn. Sybil Moholy-Nagy's slide lectures in the history of architecture particularly impressed him: "She'd turn out the lights – you couldn't take notes – and show slides of all sorts of things, rapid-fire. A Ming vase, the Acropolis, a city street, a forest, a train station. She'd talk about anything that came to mind, drawing amazing parallels. You came out of class in a daze."[4]

During his years at Pratt he participated in various student theater productions, designed sets for the dance and performance works of friends, and made an experimental film, *Slant.*

For the rest of the decade Wilson held various teaching positions in the New York City area: special instructor for public school children in Harlem with reading difficulties; physical therapist to brain-damaged children; consultant and teacher for Headstart; coordinator of theater programs for pre-schoolers, paraplegics, and iron-lung patients in city hospitals.

1964

Wilson went to the American Center in Paris to study painting with George McNeil, an American abstract expressionist on faculty at Pratt. In Germany he saw the international arts festival "documenta III" at Kassel, and attended the Wagner festival at Bayreuth.

1965

Wilson designed the sets and the grotesque plastic doll costumes worn by the three protagonists in the off-Broadway production of Jean-Claude van Itallie's *America, Hurrah!*

Jearnine Wagner (artist, teacher, actress) invited him to direct summer classes in painting and in movement at the "Ideas in Motion" Youth Theater Seminar, Trinity University, San Antonio, Texas. People from these workshops performed Wilson's *Modern Dance* at the Waco Civic Theater; the last of the four dances was a spoof on the Miss America contest, with detergent cartons as props, and a sound track medley of patriotic songs, gospel hymns and the Miss America theme song. In the local paper (*Waco Tribune Herald,* July 25) Gynter Quill profiled the twenty-three-year-old: "It is too early yet to even guess what will become of Robert Wilson, particularly since he himself isn't sure. He may be an architect who paints or produces experimental films, or he may be a producer who turns to interior architecture when he wants to eat." Quill described Wilson's plans for his first film: "It will tell the story of one person, a young girl (Jearnine Wagner, in San Antonio), alone in a contemporary world, who tries to communicate but can't. It will make extensive use of Texas landscapes, for they play a distinct part in it, help to tell the story." During Wilson's first year at Pratt, Quill reported, Martha Graham's modern dance so excited him that he wrote to her and won permission to sit in on her classes. Wilson was struck by the fact that "both the music and the dance speak for themselves, play their own distinctive part, are closely integrated yet independent. Her work had the Japanese concept of 'shibui' – strength, simplicity, individuality, and the total absence of artificiality." Describing his own emerging approach to art, Wilson said, "What I am doing – in painting, design, dance, electronic music – are happenings. Very few are predetermined. They have an order and a time limit, yes, perhaps even a rough outline, but

what happens just happens. When painting I let the paint take over … The response is emotional instead of rational."

1966

Wilson graduated at the bottom of his class at Pratt with the degree of Bachelor of Fine Arts in interior design.

At the Arcosanti Foundation in Scottsdale, Arizona, he worked for six weeks with Paolo Soleri, the visionary architect committed to designing ecologically responsible urban communities. During a brief return to Waco he suffered a nervous breakdown when he could not proceed with his painting; after a suicide attempt he was committed to a mental institution for several months.

1967

Wilson moved into a New York loft at 147 Spring Street, whose former occupants were the Open Theatre, founded in 1963, under the direction of Joseph Chaikin. In November he gave five performances of his solo piece *Baby Blood* in this loft. Wilson's first entry into the candle-lit space was accompanied by Bob Dylan's electrified blues song "Maggie's Farm;" wearing only a T-shirt he made a teetering walk across an elevated plank, using a giant lollipop as a balancing stick.

1968

In honor of his Texas dance teacher, Wilson named the group that developed around him the Byrd Hoffman School of Byrds. He appeared in two productions by avant-garde dancer Kenneth King, and performed a duet, "Alley Cats," in Meredith Monk's *Co-op.* King appeared in both versions of Wilson's *Theatre Activity.* Jerome Robbins gave him financial support, and invited him to teach movement in his American Theater Laboratory. A regular Thursday night open house at the Byrd studio was devoted to free-form group dancing.

During a summer stay at Grailville, a Catholic retreat in Loveland, Ohio, he designed and supervised the construction of *Poles* – "a theater sculpture play environment" in an open field: 676 used telephone poles were arranged in a twenty-six-foot square with a uniformly stepped ascent from two and a half to eighteen-and-a-half feet above ground. Working with local farm people, Wilson created independent theater activities in Grailville's converted barn.

Performance of *The King of Spain,* 1969.
Courtesy of Byrd Hoffman Foundation.

He began to teach art and movement classes for adults at Summit (New Jersey) Art Center, and provided the following names as a reading list: George Ivanovitch Gurdjieff (1872–1949), Armenian explorer, mystic, and cultist; Gertrude Stein (1874–1946), American writer; Isadora Duncan (1878–1927), American dancer and reformer for natural body movement; Jill Johnston (1929), American author and critic; Angela Davis (1944), American black activist and professor; Susanne K. Langer (1895), American philosopher and professor; The National Enquirer, American muckraking tabloid; Ernst Cassirer (1874–1945), German philosopher; Harry Houdini (1874–1926), American magician; Edgar Cayce (1877–1945), American clairvoyant and healer. This classic late-1960s list captures the characteristic range and unusual complexion of Wilson's interests: individual growth through self-awareness, personal expression, and a quest for mystical truths; a humanist stand against social repression; a sly attitude toward the theatrical excesses of late-capitalist popular culture.

Wilson adopted Raymond Andrews, a deaf-mute eleven-year-old black child whom he saw being harassed by a policeman on the street in Summit. Since Andrews knew no words Wilson was convinced that he thought in his own language of visual signs and symbols; he encouraged Andrews to communicate through drawings. In an attempt to learn his pre-verbal mode of communication and his body language, the members of the School of Byrds copied Andrews's gestures and sounds in movement workshops. [Andrews left the Byrds in 1973 and went to school for the first time.]

The two parts of the performance *BYRD woMAN* were presented at different sites: in the Spring Street loft and outdoors on Jones Alley in New York. Reviewing the first part, Jill Johnston wrote: "[The setting involved] a hay-covered floor [in a space] fitted out with horizontal wires (about chest height) and a couple of low boards suspended on low boxes. Bob as Byrdwoman appeared [to the fanfare of the *2001* ape music] seated in ecstatic profile outside the window on the fire escape. The rest of the piece was very quiet and pastoral. About eight people, including a young boy [Raymond Andrews] and an older lady, stood about in the hay [while] two people bounced up and down, lightly, on the boards. Bob himself looking maybe like an itinerant hobo in drag [performed] some beautiful weird maneuvering ... across the hay space and through the other relatively static performers ... His progress was stop and go in a spastic rhythm."[5]

1969

The Byrd Hoffman Foundation, a non-profit organization, was established to produce projects by Wilson and other Byrds.

In January he assembled a cast of 45 non-professionals (Byrds and people from his body-awareness classes) and rented The Anderson, a run-down vaudeville theater on the Lower East Side for two performances of *The King of Spain.* Instinct drew him to the illusionistic devices of nineteenth-century theater when creating pictures for the stage. In particular he wanted to work in an old-fashioned theater, with a stage framed by a proscenium arch: this architectural element contains and distances the image for the viewer, giving freer rein to the imagination. The set, whose *trompe l'oeil* backdrops were painted by Fred Koluch (now Kolo) depicted a musty Victorian drawing room. A central high-backed chair was turned away from the audience to face a doorway; in it sat an indistinct red-haired figure, presumed to be the king. To the left a floor-to-ceiling strip cut from the wall revealed a sunny landscape with distant mountains and sea. Entering through the door, a great variety of people slowly assembled. Eventually they filed out behind the 30-foot-high legs of what was imagined to be a gigantic cat crossing the stage. At the last moment the King broke his motionless vigil by standing and turning; the

audience saw his hairy paws (reminiscent of those in Cocteau's film *Beauty and the Beast*) and a grotesque mask face. In his review, Stephen Smoliar wrote: "Ranging in age from seven to seventy, [the cast] spent an hour being interesting by being themselves. Completely unaware of the presence of an audience, three men involved themselves in moving geometrical objects about a chess board, one woman decorated herself with black feathers, and another woman talked incessantly about all sorts of nothing ... It might go well in a museum room, where one could walk in, stand around for a while, go look at something else, and come back later to see if anything new was happening."[6]

In December Wilson worked at the Brooklyn Academy of Music for the first time, staging two performances of *The Life and Times of Sigmund Freud,* a four-hour "hybrid dance play" in three acts, with incidental music and sound effects. Act II was a shortened and reworked version of *The King of Spain.* Richard Foreman wrote in the *Village Voice:* "[It] proceeds as a series of 'tableaux vivants,' in silence or against occasional sound backgrounds. *[Act I:]* a beach scene with real sand. [People] start slowly crossing the stage, performing simple activities like sowing seed, running, crawling over the sand, [as if] the building blocks of life are laid out for us ... Freud and his wife walk across the sand, and what is slowly developed is a profound sense of the true rhythm of life, [built] not through the exercising of the will in moments of crisis and decision, but in the slow accretions that are spun around the human animal as his body and mind chew and re-chew on the materials of his mental and physical space. [The act] ends with one of the performance's many fantastic images: [Wilson] as an over-stuffed black mammy – suddenly, fantastic! – joined by a chorus of 20 or 30 over-stuffed mammies (they look like birds with puffed-out bosoms and asses) and they all shuffle over the sand as the sky darkens. *[Act III:]* wild animals slowly enter a cave [and] iron bars slowly fall over the cave opening, separating animals from the world outside [where] half-naked boys and girls run, exercise, and play. Finally Freud enters, sits at a little table amidst the resting wild beasts, and a small boy cries at his feet. [It] is slow and gigantic and wonderful, and the emotion that arises in viewing this 20th-century nativity scene is not the emotion that the theater usually evokes (those

Raymond Andrews in *Deafman Glance,* 1970.
Photo by Robert P. Marks.

Sheryl Sutton in *Deafman Glance* (Prologue), 1970.
Photo by Martin Bough.

emotions that bind us ever more firmly to what we have been conditioned to be). [Having the] whole *spectrum* of feeling awakened in us is the freedom-bestowing aim of art on the highest level."[7]

"I no longer know the difference between theatre and dance and art," wrote John Perreault in his review, calling the piece "a beautiful artwork, no matter what the category. [It] had so little obvious meaning that it contained all meanings... It was static yet full of activities. The arrangement of the incidents was musical rather than literary... I don't know how Wilson managed to manage so many people – fat people, skinny people, old people, children, all 'real' people and not stage people – and so much theatrical machinery. *[Freud]* was like a cross between [Maurice] Maeterlinck, [Alfred] Jarry, William Blake, and Raymond Roussel and yet it was totally original. It was one of the strangest things I have ever seen in my life."[8]

1970
In December the Byrds performed a new seven-hour piece at the University of Iowa, Iowa City. Titled *Deafman Glance,* it was a series of silent pictures and stories inspired by the drawings of Raymond Andrews. Many scenes took place around a hut in a forest, with Andrews present as a country youth with a fishing rod, sometimes seated on a bench

suspended high above the stage. Wilson talks about *Deafman Glance* as the culmination of his approach to the major issues then confronting alternative theater: a determination not to impose on either text or characters the intentional resolution of the narrative tradition; a belief that words are not inherently more important than light, space, and movement, and that performers may be considered as compositional elements; and an attempt to topple distinctions between art and life by incorporating activities that happen as real events in real time (as opposed to an illusionistically telescoped narrative).

Since the mid 1960s many new talents involved in performance art in New York (Yvonne Rainer, Jack Smith, and Richard Schechner, for example) addressed these issues, and their materials and processes overlapped, despite the individuality of their final statements. In lectures Wilson sometimes overlooks his peers when considering the ultimate influences on his formal deployment of space, silence, and slowness to liberate the viewer's imagination. He positions his work in relation to the achievements of the previous generation: the dance of George Balanchine and of Merce Cunningham, and the music and writings of John Cage.

Deafman Glance received French Critics Award for Best Foreign Play.

113

1971

Deafman Glance was performed at the Brooklyn Academy of
Music, and then traveled to Nancy, Rome, Paris, Amsterdam.
The tour was organized by Ninon Karlweiss, the agent who
took The Living Theater (Julian Beck's and Judith Malina's
avant-garde, politically active communal theater group) to
Europe in the 1960s. *Deafman Glance* was a sensation in
France, earning Wilson the support of such public figures as
playwright Eugène Ionesco, actor Jean-Louis Barrault,
designer Pierre Cardin, arts commissioner Michel Guy and
agent-manager Bénédicte Pesle. Louis Aragon wrote a review,
published on the front page of a communist arts weekly, that
took the form of a long letter of reconciliation to his dead
surrealist colleague, André Breton. "I have never seen anything
more beautiful in the world. [Theater] has never come close to
this, which is simultaneously life awake and life with closed
eyes, the confusion between the everyday world and the world
of night, reality mixed with a dream, everything inexplicable to
the eyes of a deafman... Some call it low-grade or shopwindow
surrealism, [but] this is not surrealism at all. [It is what we,] from
whom surrealism was born, dreamed it would become after us,
beyond us. [How] exalted you would be at virtually every
moment of this masterpiece of surprise. [This] strange spectacle, neither ballet, nor mime, nor opera (but perhaps a deaf
opera) calls forth new ways with light and shadow. [It] seems to
criticize everything we do out of habit. *[Deafman Glance]* is an
extraordinary freedom machine."[9]

Wilson was awarded a Guggenheim Fellowship for 1971–72.

In the fall, Wilson wrote for several weeks in a cabin in British
Columbia, Canada.

Deafman Glance received New York Drama Desk Award for
Direction.

1972

Wilson was invited to make a work for the Shiraz arts festival in
Iran. The central themes of the new piece were explored in
*Overture for KA MOUNTAIN AND GUARDenia TERRACE,
a story about a family and some people changing,* first
performed in the Byrd Hoffman Studio in April. Edwin Denby,
author and former dance critic of *The Herald Tribune,* took part
in the production.

Wilson's mother died in May.

Imprisoned on Crete for possession of hashish in July, Wilson
was released on bail, and joined the Byrds in Shiraz. Rehearsals
were underway for *KA MOUNTAIN AND GUARDenia
TERRACE,* their main contribution to the festival. This seven-
day continuous event, presented in September on the seven
hills of the Haft-tan Mountain, included the following: thirty
members of the School of Byrds; twenty Iranian recruits; a
menagerie of live animals and birds; sculptures of flamingos,
and pasteboard models of bearded old men, Noah's ark, a
whale, and a dinosaur. The troup journeyed from peak to peak
like pilgrims, gradually ascending to the highest mountain.
Performing on a platform stage or directly in the landscape,
they employed rudimentary props to suggest such settings as a
jail, a suburban housing development, a Wild West saloon, the
Acropolis, a missile site, the New York skyline, a Chinese
pagoda.

Describing *Overture for KA MOUNTAIN* as presented in the
Narenjestan Garden, Shiraz, Basil Langton wrote: "[By] some
mysterious alchemy [the performance] captured the spirit of
modern art. I have never felt the work of Magritte or Dubuffet
in the theater before, nor the sculpture of Giacometti... Everything was larger than life and often extremely theatrical. They
employed mask, dance, mime, symbol – all elements of the
classic theater tradition – and the verbal and visual images
were more often sur-real than real. Yet in spite of this super-
natural un-reality, there was no sense of anything being
performed. Everything seemed merely to exist, in its own time,
its own shape, and its own dimension... [The Byrds have]
developed a discipline and technique of their own that allows
them to do things with astonishing control and refinement."[10]

In November the Byrd Hoffman School of Byrds presented
Overture for KA MOUNTAIN AND GUARDenia TERRACE in
Paris. There were two parts: a six-day exhibition of dances,
texts, objects and music at the Musée Galliéra and a twenty-
four-hour performance at the Opéra-Comique. .

1973

The Byrd Hoffman Foundation bought wilderness land in
British Columbia for an educational summer retreat. During

Performance of *KA MOUNTAIN
AND GUARDenia TERRACE,
a story about a family and some
people changing,* Shiraz, 1972.

Photos (top row) Basil Langton, Bahman Djalali;
(middle and bottom rows) Bahman Djalali.

their first visit a suspicious neighbor informed the Mounties about a hippie drug ring, but a raid produced only a few joints.

At the Det Ny Theater, Copenhagen, Denmark, and then the Brooklyn Academy of Music, Wilson presented *The Life and Times of Joseph Stalin,* a compilation of his work since 1969. It began at 7 p.m. and ran continuously for twelve hours. The cast of about 140 included Wilson's eighty-seven-year-old grandmother, Mrs. Alma Hamilton, who appeared in the first three acts, then slept in a dressing room from midnight until the end of the piece the next morning. There were seven acts – Beach; Victorian Drawing Room; Cave; Forest; Temple; Victorian Bedroom; Planet. Wilson created a degree of structural symmetry by building parallels into the settings or actions of acts 1 and 7, 2 and 6, and 3 and 5. Act 4 was thus the center, and at its midpoint he staged the death by poisoning of Stalin's first wife. Because Stalin had kept two identical apartments, each with an armchair draped in white fabric, his wife's death was witnessed on stage by two identically costumed Stalin figures (played by Wilson and Cindy Lubar) seated in identical draped armchairs. Adjusted to incorporate references to Stalin, this piece re-presented many of Wilson's earlier works. For example, Act 4 was derived from *Deafman Glance.* Only the last act featured new material, most notably a dance for thirty-two ostriches.

Discussing *Stalin* in The *New York Times,* Edwin Denby wrote: [The] content of Wilson's pieces is that of images, and I would like to call it visionary in that sense. And I think it was meant that way. It can be translated into psychological or narrative terms, into words, but it doesn't have to be. It can be taken directly as the images and pictures, as something that keeps changing in that sense like a dream… Sometimes, later on, you know what a dream means. And sometimes you don't. But usually you don't. But at any rate, while its going on, you don't ask… The idea that you can understand it only if you can verbalize it is what I don't think is true or useful. And that is unfortunately usually done by people trying to tell each other what happened [in Wilson's silent operas]… What you can't describe is the logical narrative connection. And the psychological connection. But you don't have to describe that. That's not what he's showing you. It might be that later on he would. Since his work adds so much from year to year."[11]

Robert Wilson in rehearsal for *Life and Times of Joseph Stalin,* 1973. Photos by Carl Paler. Photos courtesy of Byrd Hoffman Foundation.

Life and Times of Joseph Stalin, Brooklyn Academy of Music, 1973.
Photo courtesy of Byrd Hoffman Foundation. Photo by Carl Paler.

Advertisement, *Village Voice*, 1973.

T.E. Kalem wrote in *Time Magazine:* "[*Stalin*] is a labyrinthine dream from which one cannot awaken, a slow-motion time study that makes the slow motion of, say, film or videotape seem like a device of dizzying speed. Wilson's imagination is hallucinatory, evoking the visions of drug takers. [In the prologue to Act 4] a slim young black mother, dressed in black … wakes one of her nightgowned small children, pours and serves a glass of milk, then slays the child ritually with a glittering silver knife. She wakes the other child and repeats the action. Then she grieves for both with the same grave serenity with which she has killed them. Wilson can also be funny. He mixes Gertrude Stein gibberish with high camp and low burlesque. One of the show's running gags is just that – a fellow in a red shirt and shorts who jogs rapidly across the back of the stage at intervals, always meticulously identical in pace. At times this makes for sheer absurdity; at other times it seems almost like a mystical trance."[12]

In the first minutes of *Stalin*, Wilson performed a spontaneous dialogue with Christopher Knowles, a brain-damaged fourteen-year-old attending a state-funded school of mental health in Schenectady, New York. Prior to Stalin, Wilson had heard a tape-recording made by Knowles, called *Emily likes the TV*, in which he created arrangements of words by re-recording segments from a tape of himself speaking. Wilson was struck by the way Knowles's quasi-musical sense of pattern and geometrical structure paralleled his own: "[Christopher] was not afraid to destroy the word. The language was really alive. [Words] were always growing and changing … like molecules bursting apart into all directions all the time. It was really three-dimensional, like space or something."[13] Recognizing Wilson's success in communicating with their son, Knowles's parents eventually allowed Christopher to move to the Spring Street loft of the Byrd School.

1974

In March, Wilson and Knowles made the first of their *DIA LOG* pieces, *A MAD MAN A MAD GIANT A MAD DOG A MAD URGE A MAD FACE:* improvisatory performances in which they repeated in turn the Dada-esque fragments of Knowles's sound poems and texts and followed a sequence of movements.

Five different *DIA LOG* works were made and performed internationally through 1980.

In April *Stalin* was performed in São Paulo as *The Life and Times of Dave Clark*; in deference to the political climate in Brazil Wilson substituted the name of a Canadian criminal.

The demands of marshalling voluntary communal effort on the massive scale of *Stalin* led Wilson to create a streamlined three-hour work for a cast of eleven: *A Letter for Queen Victoria*. It premiered in Spoleto, Italy, in May, and toured to nine more European cities before a three-week run on Broadway in April 1975. Alan Lloyd composed chamber music for string quartet, flute, and contralto. A script of speeches and dialogues by Wilson and his associates was published. For the first time in a large production, words – however unintelligible by conventional standards – had a conspicuous presence. Knowles had inspired this change in Wilson's work. While increasingly engaged with words Wilson was careful to subvert any normal usage. He patterned them architecturally on the script page (reminiscent of John Cage's experiments in his 1961 anthology *Silence*), hoping that in experiencing the spoken text the audience would sense the words losing their familiar meanings as their sounds became more transparent. Laurence Shyer suggested that the backdrop in *Queen Victoria* showing a dam with words rushing through its cracked barrier wall symbolized the torrent of language loosed in this work; he noted that Wilson once compared the curing of his stutter and his conquest of speech to "a dam bursting."[14]

From a Knowles text used in A Letter for Queen Victoria:

THE SUNDANCE KID WAS BEAUTIFUL
THE SUNDANCE KID DANCED A LOT
THE SUNDANCE KID DANCED AROUND THE ROOM
RAISING RAISING
RAISE RACE RACING
THE SUNDANCE KID RAISE DANCE RACE
DANCE DANCING
RAISE RAISING
RACE RACING
YEAH THE SUNDANCE KID COULD DANCE A LOT

Christopher Knowles in *Dialog/Curious George*, 1980.
Photo by Leo Van Velzen.

Robert Wilson and Christopher Knowles in *Dialog/Network*, 1977.
Photo by Babette Mangolte.

In *Queen Victoria* painted illusionistic drops gave way to spare and virtually monochromatic sets. Much of the imagery alluded to the triangular shape of an envelope's flap, which was recalled by the tautly extended train of a dress, a slide projection of a pointed shirt collar, and the slanting triangles of light beams hitting the wall and floor. This use of a recurring visual geometry exemplified Wilson's larger turn towards a minimalist aesthetic, which became increasingly evident as the decade progressed.

The creation of *Queen Victoria* precipitated the end of the Byrd School as a collaborative group and marked Wilson's move to assume a professional identity and an authorial voice. In earlier productions, the Byrds had all worked together, everyone ending up with an activity; *Queen Victoria* was the first piece to be cast by audition, and some of the Byrds were embittered by exclusion.

In September Wilson created the first exhibition of his sculpture and drawings at the Musée Galliéra, Paris.

The Life and Times of Joseph Stalin received Obie Special Award Citation for Direction.

A Letter for Queen Victoria was recorded for television by The Byrd Hoffman Foundation.

1975

The $ Value of Man, written and directed with Christopher Knowles, was presented at the Brooklyn Academy of Music in May; the audience sat on bleachers on all four sides of the performance space. Arnold Aronson reviewed it as follows: "[A] piece filled with parodistic and caricatured images of money, greed, and commerce. [After] the lush scenic imagery, grandiose staging and spectacle of Wilson's recent 'operas,' this marked a definite change: [it used] an arena-type stage and encouraged the audience to move about as it pleased. [The] staging was ostensibly simple with a greater emphasis on verbal and visual imagery. [The work] was divided into nine sections which were repetitions, variations, and combinations of three basic motifs [designated 'free' (dancing), 'vaudeville,' and 'casino']. For most sections the playing area was divided into halves or quarters either by drops and partitions or merely through acting use... The lights were shuttered so as to project

square, rather than round, areas of light... Michael Galasso's music had a symmetrical element, being written in sections of four, six, or eight minutes [and using] two motifs – the 'trance' music of the free and casino sections, and the lighter, up-beat, though equally hypnotic vaudeville music that had its roots in such composers as Hoagy Carmichael." [15]

The second DIA LOG by Christopher Knowles and Wilson premiered at the American Dance Festival, Connecticut College, New London.

Wilson received a Playwrighting Fellowship from the Rocke-feller Foundation.

A Letter for Queen Victoria received the Maharam Award for best set design for a Broadway show and the Tony nomination for best score and lyrics.

1976

In January, Wilson collaborated with artist Ralph Hilton to produce the video installation work *Spaceman* at The Kitchen Center for Video and Music, New York. A long, framed structure (twelve feet by three and one half feet by sixty-five feet), covered by transparent plastic, contained more than twenty video monitors, props, and Hilton as a silent seated performer.

In February Christopher Knowles and Wilson premiered their third DIA LOG at the Whitney Museum, New York.

In March the Iolas Gallery mounted the first New York exhibition of Wilson's sculptures and drawings.

Wilson's growing desire to work with dance, music, and theater professionals was fulfilled by *Einstein on the Beach,* an opera in four acts by Robert Wilson and Philip Glass, with choreography by Andrew de Groat. The thirty-six member cast, including Sheryl Sutton and Lucinda Childs, performed without interruption for five hours. *Einstein* premiered in July at the Festival d'Avignon, then traveled to Hamburg, Paris, Belgrade, Venice, Brussels, Rotterdam, and finally to New York for two sold-out performances in November. The production costs (including rental of the Metropolitan Opera, New York) left Wilson's Byrd Hoffman Foundation $ 121,000 in debt.

Einstein was a loud, intense, minutely detailed spectacle. Although fueled by the universal Western mythologies of

Albert Einstein as mathematical genius, violin-player, and humble shaggy-haired dreamer in baggy pants, the work resisted conclusive interpretations. Einstein the man and Einstein the figurehead of the atomic age could be constructed in the viewer's mind from the many fragments and clues provided on stage. Because movement, light, decor, text, and music were separately conceived and created by various collaborators, each had its own formal independence and internal structure. However, when performed simultaneously, their interactions shifted between concerted, arbitrary, and disjunctive effects. As a result, people had diverse reactions to the same moment, since many concurrent actions competed for their attention.

Wilson structured *Einstein* as a repeating sequence of three different kinds of space. The entr'actes (known as "Knee Plays," because they served as joints between the acts) were performed in front of the stage curtain in a very shallow, close-up space that he thought of in terms of portraiture. The sets for the scenes showing a train, a building, a courtroom, and a prison cell gave these objects the intermediate depth of field common in still-life composition. And finally, the sets that provided maximum space for dance groups – the open field and the massive spaceship interior – had the depth of landscape. For the first time Wilson laid out the sequence of scenic compositions in a sketchbook, which functioned both as a storyboard and as a diagram of the rhymes and repetitions within the work's underlying visual form.

In his 1978 essay, "Theater in the Age of Einstein: The Crack in the Chimney," Robert Brustein wrote, "All of Wilson's bizarre theatre pieces involve a relativity-influenced temporal and spatial sense. [His latest work] shows the influence of Einstein both in its physics and its spirit. [Every performer] has been made up [in suspenders, gray pants, and tennis shoes] to resemble Einstein... [The] work dramatizes (so subtly one absorbs it through the imagination rather than the mind) the change in perception – especially perception of time – that accompanied [our] technological development [from the locomotive to the spaceship]. The interminable length of the performance, therefore, becomes a condition of its theme, as do the strange schematic settings, the vertical and horizontal shafts of lights, and the apparently meaningless snatches of

dialogue.... Wilson is beginning to fashion some very powerful visual metaphors which have been surpassed, I believe, only in the movie that obviously influenced *Einstein on the Beach* – namely, Stanley Kubrick's *2001*. It is true that the visual effects are the most dazzling and original aspects of the work: Wilson is essentially a painter who paints in motion."[16]

In December more than fifty drawings related to *Einstein on the Beach* constituted Wilson's first solo exhibition at the Paula Cooper Gallery, New York.

Einstein on the Beach received French Critics Award for best musical theater, Belgrade International Theater Festival Grand Prize, and Lumen Award for Design.

1977
Wilson wrote and performed in the two-act, two-character play *I was sitting on my patio this guy appeared I thought I was hallucinating*. He and Lucinda Childs toured the piece in the United States and Europe between April 1977 and June 1978. The script comprised two almost identical forty-five minute monologues. Wilson recited the first alone on stage, and Childs did the same for the second act. During each act different slides and movies were shown on a small screen hung just under the proscenium arch (the projected images included words as well as penguins, ducks, a spaniel on a rumpled bed, and airport baggage inspection X-rays). Body microphones worn by the performers detached their voices from their stage presences and amplified them from other points in the theater. A third "character" was the electrified voice of an unseen male (whose lines punctuated each monologue in an effect similar to Richard Foreman's use of an unseen narrator).

Wilson wrote about *Patio:* "The language I wrote [in my notebook for the piece] was more a reflection of the way we think than of the way we normally speak. My head became like a TV, switching from thought to thought (and in writing from phrase to phrase) like flipping a dial from channel to channel. I write best when I am alone and there are no interruptions. I sometimes keep a television on at low volume and incorporate phrases I hear into my text, which I write quickly, usually leaving it untouched and in its original order once the words are on the page."[17]

Writing in *Kansas Quarterly*, Luis O. Arata said, "Neither Wilson nor his speech seemed to go anywhere. On the contrary, [it was a continual] stream of unrelated but familiar phrases. [However,] after Childs began her monologue and it became evident that she was repeating what Wilson had already said, the play, in a most simply way, gained a new dimension. Now one could hear something heard before and remembered in a fragmentary way. The performance was repeating itself, yet it was a quite different experience: now the disconnected monologue had a clear referent – Wilson's monologue – which remained in the spectator's memory as a confusing event witnessed before. [Repetition] conferred a strong sense of order to a text which was still chaotic."[18]

I was sitting on my patio this guy appeared I thought I was hallucinating, 1977.
Photos by Nathanial Tilestone.

Christopher Knowles and Wilson premiered DIA LOG/ NETWORK in October at Spazio Teatro Sperimentale, Florence.

In November the Multiples/Goodman gallery in New York presented a Wilson exhibition titled "Furniture" (also shown at the Galerie Folker Skulima, Berlin, in May 1978). He transformed nine furniture designs for the stage into independent sculptural objects; he also produced his first prints (a series of ten intaglios of furniture imagery) for Multiples/Goodman.

1978

In Paris, Wilson made *Video 50,* a 50-minute film for television
(produced by Film/Video Collectif, Lausanne, and ZDF, the
German television station). The work consists of 30-second
episodes, which include such repeating scenarios as a door
closing, Wilson in a suit at the edge of a waterfall, a chair
suspended before a dramatic sky, a leather-jacketed youth
smoking under a naked light bulb, a little girl on a swing in a
forest.

1979

*Death, Destruction, and Detroit (An Opera with Music in 2 Acts.
A Love Story in 16 Scenes)* was created for Peter Stein's theater
company Schaubühne am Halleschen Ufer, Berlin. Wilson
worked for the first time with Hans Peter Kuhn, the company's
sound engineer. The piece was more than five hours long.

Although never identified as a character or even mentioned in
the script, Rudolf Hess was the underlying focus. In the form of
seemingly innocuous images, facts, and quotes, Wilson imper-
ceptibly threaded Hitler's deputy (still at that time alive in
nearby Spandau prison) through the work: an aviator in
goggles, a parachutist, a prisoner too distracted and proud to
put more than a minimum of effort into raking the prison yard, a
Nazi dinosaur facing extinction.

Comments by Wilson about *Death Destruction and Detroit:* "I
was more extravagant [with lighting] than I've ever been. I did
things like paint a white line on a [man's hand holding a rake],
then light one side with a warm light and the other with a cold
light. I don't know anyone else who's doing that in theater.
Visconti did beautiful lighting at one time [and] in still photo-
graphy there's Horst, [who] spends three hours to light a face
with three lamps ... The lighting in Scene 9 came from a
photograph of [Albert Speer's] Nuremburg staging. There are
eighty lights on the floor, parallel beams that point straight up.
It makes a wall of light ... The text is structured like music,
[and] used like a score. For example, [Scene 1 has] A, B, C, and
D parts. Part A is spoken very rapidly and matter of fact, like a
news broadcaster who just reports with no emotion, [as is part
D. But parts] B and C have more color and texture and feeling.
This textual material repeats throughout the whole piece; it's
like a seed."[19]

Eugène Ionesco and Robert Wilson, 1978.
Courtesy of Byrd Hoffman Foundation.

DIA LOG/CURIOUS GEORGE, the fifth and last of Wilson's
collaborative performances with Christopher Knowles, premiered in Brussels in April, then toured internationally in 1980.

Edison, A Play in Four Acts, previewed in New York and was
presented in Lyon, Milan, and Paris. Again Wilson used a
historical figure (Thomas Edison, the American inventor of the
incandescent electric lamp) as the animus for a densely woven
sequence of theatrical images. He relied on Maita di Niscemi,
who had researched the historical figures and contributed texts
to *Death Destruction and Detroit,* to provide the biographical
materials about Edison and his friend Henry Ford.

Death, Destruction, and Detroit received the German Critics
Award for best play of the season.

1980

Robert Stearns organized the exhibition and catalogue *Robert
Wilson: The Theater of Images* (shown at the Contemporary
Arts Center, Cincinnati, and the Neuberger Museum, State
University of New York at Purchase. The exhibition, wrote
Craig Owens, was "a series of profoundly arresting tableaux

The Man in the Raincoat, Cologne, 1981.
Photos by Friedemann Simon.

that engaged the viewer directly, without reference to their theatrical origins... The spectator became a participant in a kind of ritual procession to a consecrated site. The effectiveness of [these] images within the museum context was largely the result of Wilson's determination to use its galleries as more than neutral containers for isolated objects... [He] worked to transform the museum into a theater of encounters. A major factor in this transformation – and in all of Wilson's work – was light."[20]

Wilson attended the Bayreuth Festival as the guest of Wolfgang Wagner, and saw the Patrice Chereau-Pierre Boulez production of the Ring cycle and other Wagner operas (including *Parsifal*). Although preliminary discussions took place with Bayreuth, Wilson's first invitation to produce an opera came soon afterwards from Giancarlo de Monaco of the Kassel State Opera: *Parsifal* was chosen, and Wilson began work on visualizing a scenic design in which the Temple of the Holy Grail is envisioned as an enormous disc-like ring of light that flies through the sky and floats on the lake.

Wilson received a Guggenheim Fellowship.

1981

In February at the Biennial Exhibition of the Whitney Museum of American Art, New York, Wilson installed as a stage set the three pieces of stainless steel furniture and the painted stage drops from *I was sitting on my patio this guy appeared I thought I was hallucinating.*

In February at the Music Theater Lab, Kennedy Center, Washington, D.C., Wilson directed a workshop performance in preparation for a new work about Medea.

The Man in the Raincoat, a new solo work with designs by Wilson and a sound piece by Hans Peter Kuhn, was performed twice at an international theater festival in Cologne in June. One scene involved twenty-five extras dressed like Wilson.

In June, three months before the scheduled premiere of *Parsifal,* the Kassel State Opera broke its contract with Wilson. This production has not yet been realized.

At a nine-day workshop for performers, composers, researchers, and technicians in Munich, in August, Wilson outlined *the CIVIL warS: a tree is best measured when it is down,* a work to be the opening event of the 1984 Olympic Arts Festival in Los Angeles. This was to be a twelve-hour opera in five acts and a suite of short entr'actes (again referred to as "Knee Plays," as they had been in *Einstein on the Beach*) performed on a small stage during set changes. It would be constructed in six countries (West Germany, Holland, France, Italy, Japan, and the U.S.A.) and its parts performed together for the first time at the Olympic Games. This new epic, and a commitment to secure a large share of its funding, preoccupied Wilson through April 1984. His initial thoughts about the project developed from his study of Matthew Brady's photographs documenting the American Civil War. But soon the theme of unity and disunity was massively extended in historical and cultural scope, and came to include domestic strife, the geological theory of continental drift, and shifting relations between Japan and the West.

In New York Wilson directed the production of the video piece *Deafman Glance,* a 27-minute version of the murder scene first presented as the prologue to the fourth act of *Deafman Glance.* Sheryl Sutton, who introduced the role on stage, appeared in the production.

Wilson designed the lighting and decor for Lucinda Childs's *Relative Calm,* a work for nine dancers (presented in Strasbourg, Bordeaux, Nice, Grenoble, Brooklyn).

Wilson received a three-year grant from the Rockefeller Foundation.

Wilson's father died.

1982
Die Goldenen Fenster [The Golden Windows], a play in three parts, was written by Wilson and presented at the Münchner Kammerspiele, Munich. The text recalled that of *Patio* in its cryptic and fragmented style and its scrambled references to guns and murder. There were four speaking parts: Man on the Bench (played by Peter Lühr), Woman in Black Dress (played by Maria Nicklisch), Man on the Rope, Woman in White Dress. The set was an obelisk-like house on a mountain, viewed at a different time of night (evening, midnight, approaching dawn) in each part. David Warrilow, who played Man on the Bench in the 1985 Brooklyn Academy of Music Production), has said, "The imagery of *The Golden Windows* is inevitable, the

Jessye Norman in *Great Day in the Morning,*
Théâtre des Champs Elysées, Paris, 1982
Photo by Leo Van Velzen.

language floats around that imagery in a way that is not satisfactorily grounded and inevitable ... [Bob] was very, very specific about the last words of the piece which are simply 'it alright.' [The last line is: 'it is now dawn well i didn't have any choice it alright'.] So my job was to drain any expression out of my face, to turn around blank and receptive to what the audience wanted to put there. For 'it' he asked for a lightening of the voice to suggest the semblance of a question mark and a slow turn, looking in a particular way toward the light. By the time I said 'alright' there was no decision on the part of the actor as to what was really being said. It was so close to being a question that one couldn't really take it as a statement. There was no period so the end of the piece floated ... There is in Bob's work almost an expectation of perfection. That creates a lot of stress and that's the last thing the audience should see."[21]

In October Wilson collaborated with soprano Jessye Norman to produce *A Great Day in the Morning* for the Théâtre des Champs-Elysées, Paris. The concert was Norman's selection of spirituals, songs born of oppression of black slaves in the

American South, which celebrate dignity and religious inner strength.

In New York Wilson directed the production of the videotape *Stations,* a 57-minute work with thirteen sections structured as fantastic events that befall a boy and his family in an isolated country house; several scenes recall imagery first developed in 1970 for *Deafman Glance.*

1983

The Dutch section of *the CIVIL warS* (with music by Nicolas Economou) was produced in Rotterdam in September, then toured eight French cities. The figures represented included William the Silent, Queen Wilhelmina, Mata Hari, the American giantess Anna Swann holding a midget boy (as photographed by Matthew Brady), and the characters in "Jack and the Beanstalk."

Solo exhibtions were held at Pavillon des Arts Paris, Museum Boymans-van Beuningen, Rotterdam, and Sogetsu School, Tokyo.

1984

The German section of *the CIVIL warS,* coauthored by Wilson and East German playwright Heiner Müller, was produced in Cologne in January (and presented in Berlin in May). The life of Frederick the Great was featured; other characters included two astronauts floating in space in front of a continent that splits in two, an extended family group, historic batallions of German and American soldiers, a tortoise, Frederick the Great's dog, and a pair of dancing polar bears. Hans Peter Kuhn created sound design and musical compositions. Philip Glass also contributed music.

The Italian section of *the CIVIL warS,* billed as an opera by Philip Glass and Robert Wilson, was produced in Rome in March. (Separate productions by the Netherlands Opera and the Brooklyn Academy of Music took place in 1986). The characters included Giuseppe Garibaldi, Abraham and Mary Lincoln, Robert E. Lee, and a tribe of Hopi Indians.

On the last day of March the Los Angeles Olympic Organizing Committee announced the cancellation of *the CIVIL warS* since they remained $1.2 million short of the $2.6 million budget for the world premiere.

The Knee Plays, the American contribution to *the CIVIL warS,* was produced in Minneapolis in April (subsequent productions were seen in Germany, France, Spain, Italy, the U.S.A., Japan, and Australia, 1985-88). The thirteen entr'actes tell the story of a tree that is made into a boat; the boat has many adventures and becomes the subject of a book; the knowledge that the book gives to a reader is shown when it unfolds into the image of the original tree. David Byrne (a member of the rock group Talking Heads) created music inspired by the marching bands of New Orleans, and wrote spoken lyrics for some pieces. Suzushi Hanayagi (a leading figure in Japanese classical dance) devised the movements for the performers.

In September Wilson made a new version of the 1976 installation *The Spaceman* as his contribution to the video exhibition *The Luminous Image* at the Stedelijk Museum, Amsterdam. In October at the Opéra de Lyon, France, Wilson for the first time staged the work of another artist, while undertaking the same subject for one of his own projects: he staged Marc-Antoine Charpentier's 1693 opera *Médée,* a five-act baroque lyric tragedy, succeeded on the following evening by the five-act opera *Medea,* which he had written in 1982 with English composer Gavin Bryars. Each production lasted four hours. The Wilson/Bryars piece included as a prologue the 1982 Heiner Müller text *Despoiled Shore Medeamaterial Landscape with Argonauts,* and adapted the Euripedes text for its libretto. Reviewing the Charpentier opera in the *New York Times,* John Rockwell wrote that Wilson had "created a vocabulary of stylized hand gestures and body movements, which while not authentically Baroque, recalled that period admirably. And the restraint of his scenery, punctuated by a few spectacular moments proved surprisingly appropriate. The final scene, with Medea rising ever upward until she became a 30-foot-tall totem, her robe stretched symmetrically below her like a pyramid, will remain in the mind a long time... [In the Wilson/Bryars *Medea*] the staging is even more static and classically simple, even though there are typically Wilsonian moments – a pantheon of gods and greats (Gandhi, Einstein, Buddha, Moses, Marx), a fantastic serpent chariot on which Medea descends in the final act, and the transformation of the recurrent Greek columns of the earlier scenes into pagan cat-gods at the end,

Above:

The Knee Plays 12 from *the CIVIL warS*.

Walker Art Center, Minneapolis, 1984. Photo by Jo Ann Verburg.

Right:

Robert Wilson in *Einstein on the Beach*, Brooklyn Academy of Music, 1984.

Photos by Lynn Kohlman.

figures that also lurked behind the Charpentier *Médée* at the end of that opera."[22]

In Lyons, Wilson created twenty lithographs of settings from the Wilson/Bryars *Medea.*

In December *Einstein on the Beach* was revived at the Brooklyn Academy of Music.

The Cologne section of *the CIVIL warS* won the Berlin Festspiele Theatertreffen Award. It was recorded for German television by WDR in cooperation with Köln Schauspielhaus.

1985

In February Wilson staged a variation of the German section of *the CIVIL warS* with the American Repertory Theatre, Cambridge, Massachusetts. A year later this production was the unanimous choice of the jury for the Pulitzer Prize in drama; the Pulitzer Board declined to give the award, apparently because the production was only one section of a work that had never been performed in its entirety, and because no traditional script was available for review.

The Brooklyn Academy of Music staged the first American production of *The Golden Windows* in October.

In Munich Wilson made nineteen lithographs of scenes from his unrealized production of Wagner's *Parsifal.*

1986

Wilson embarked on his second experiment with tandem productions. He wrote and staged a new work based on Euripides' Alcestis (with the Heiner Müller text *Description of a Picture/Explosion of a Memory* as a prologue and the anonymous Japanese Noh farce *The Birdcatcher in Hell* as an epilogue); and he staged Christoph Wilibald Gluck's 1776 opera *Alceste.* The pervasive eclecticism of *Alcestis* (presented by the American Repertory Theatre, Cambridge, in March) demonstrated the extent to which Wilson had benefitted from the multicultural program of *the CIVIL warS.* Elinor Fuchs acknowledged this breakthrough in her review: "On a small forestage was the sprawled figure of a man in seersucker pants (a recurring image of helplessness)... At an angle to the main stage was a shallow third stage [with] a 19-foot-high Cycladic fertility figure, a kind of androgyne, under whose gaze the performance proceeded. Before its crossed arms, in the scale of

German section of *the CIVIL warS,* American Repertory Theatre, 1985.
Photo by Richard Feldman.

infant to mother, stood a gray mummy-wrapped being, [which spoke the Müller prologue] in an inscrutable voice, neither masculine not feminine... The scrim rose to reveal a jagged mountain range, inspired by Wilson's recent visit to Delphi... At intervals, boulders inched down the rocky wall. We were not in human but in geologic time. Near the mountain stood three cypress trees. In an eyeblink they turned into classical columns: we were watching not only the planetary change of nature but the rise and fall of cultures. Later, in another sudden transformation, the columns became industrial smokestacks, which later still belched fire and appeared to melt in an internal blaze. On closer inspection Wilson's mountain, his monument of nature, revealed itself to be a tomb of culture. The wreckage of

Above:
Alcestis, American Repertory Theatre, Cambridge, 1986.
Photos by Richard Feldman.

Right:
Alceste, Staatsoper Stuttgart, 1986.
Photos by Andreas Pohlmann.

a Viking ship, Chinese funerary heads, and other formations were caught in its formations. Toward the end, a glowing 'city of the future' appeared on a peak, looking oddly like a crèche... Wilson wanted to break up the game of 'ping pong' (his word) that comes from theatrical dialogue and, more generally, from aligning words and images. [Solutions included Suzushi Hanayagi's vocabulary of formal, abstract gestures based on classical Noh dance; Hans Peter Kuhn's audio environment that ranged from the hyperrealism of bird sounds to the abstaction of Japanese flutes; John Conklin's multicultural costumes.] But Wilson is too powerful a mythmaker to settle for mere eclecticism. I was especially struck by the abundance of feminine emblems and figures in this production. In the past, Wilson's work, pace Queen Victoria, has been organized under the sign of male culture. Though often played by actresses, his 'heroes' have [included Stalin and Einstein, and] some of his subjects [were] death, destruction, and civil war. Feminists have been slow to lay claim to postmodernism, especially in works by male practitioners. Yet among its many myths of death and renewal, Wilson's *Alcestis* seemed to entertain a feminist vision that is truly postmodern: the decay of patriarchy and a return of the feminine. How eerily [it] embodied both the positive and negative postmodernisms of recent cultural theory: on the one hand, a new imaging of the relativity of our own culture and a distancing from Western master narratives partly seen through a distrust of narrative itself; on the other, a representation, arguably, of the 'story' of late capitalism – consumption – as evidenced in the tremendous proliferation of cultural signs employed for exchange value. Their value, that is, lies not in what they say about their cultures of origin (other signs from other cultures might have done just as well) but in what they 'purchase,' a subjective, immediately re-exchangeable, experience in the theater."[23]

Wilson's design for Gluck's *Alceste* (which premiered at the Württemberg State Opera, Stuttgart, in December) was stark, relatively monochromatic, and appropriately neoclassical compared with his own *Alcestis*. The principal motif was a cube: it tumbled through space, becoming larger and closer, like an omen of the death that Alcestis volunteered for to save her husband's life; a cube resting at the center of the stage

suggested her acceptance of death, and her journey to Hades became a walk into a square black void (an image which was switched instantaneously into a square of blinding white light when Heracles brought her back from the dead).

In Austin, Texas, Wilson made ten lithographs of scenes from his staging of *Alceste.*

In May Wilson staged Heiner Müller's 1977 play *Hamletmachine* with fifteen acting students from New York University (the production toured Europe in 1987). The six-page play (essentially monologues by Hamlet and Ophelia types) became a two-and-a-half-hour Wilson work. In a brief statement published in the New York production's playbill Müller observed: "When I wrote *Hamletmachine* after translating Shakespeare's Hamlet for a theater in East Berlin, it turned out to be my most American play, quoting T.S. Eliot, Andy Warhol, Coca Cola, Ezra Pound, and Susan Atkins. It may be read as a pamphlet against the illusion that one can stay innocent in this our world. I am glad that Robert Wilson does my play, his theater being a world of its own." Wilson began *Hamletmachine* by establishing his world in the silent choreography that served as a prologue, and involved multiple, differently stereotyped Ophelias and Hamlets. The actors repeated the prologue movements four times during the presentation of the text. With each repetition Wilson's spare set (a long table, chairs, and a dead tree) was rearranged to give the illusion that the room was on a machine that rotated it through quarter-turns until it had been viewed through each side.

A German production of *Hamletmachine* was made in Hamburg in October. It was recorded for German television by NDR in cooperation with Thalia Theater.

Hamletmachine received Obie Award for direction; Wilson's solo version of *Overture to the Fourth Act of Deafman Glance* received Malaga [Spain] Theater Festival Picasso Award.

1987
In January Wilson made his debut at La Scala, Milan, with a production of *Salome,* the 1905 opera by Richard Strauss (based on Oscar Wilde's play). He chose to treat the music, the acting, and the set changes as three different events taking place at the same time. Vocalists in black formal wear sang concert-style

Death Destruction and Detroit II,
Schaubühne Theater. Berlin, 1987.
Photo by Ruth Walz.

Quartet, American Repertory Theatre, Cambridge, 1988.
Photo by Richard Feldman.

from a small platform abutting stage right; performers costumed in Gianni Versace's punk couture danced and moved within the proscenium; and behind, a landscape with mountains changed its configuration independently of the singing and acting. Four differently costumed actresses (usually onstage together) suggested particular aspects of Salome: an Alice-in-Wonderland girl, a sex kitten in neglige, a femme fatale in evening gown, a classically draped seer.

In February a new four-hour work was created for the Schaubühne am Lehniner Platz in West Berlin: *Death Destruction and Detroit II.* Wilson remodeled a large auditorium, installing metal stools and support rails that gave the audience freedom to turn in any direction to view the surrounding stages. He made one deep conventional stage and filled the opposite wall with a massive stepped wall (like the wall of an Inca fortress) with narrow ledges where actors could walk and climb; in one corner a glass-sided elevator traveled from floor to ceiling beside the ledged wall; two shallow stages extended the full length of the flanking walls; a trapdoor in the ceiling allowed actors to address the audience from above. In this sequel to the 1979 *Death Destruction and Detroit* (which often alluded to Rudolf Hess), Wilson named Kafka as his central reference, widely quoting from his stories, letters, and diaries in the program book. In an extraordinary outpouring of characters on all sides – Chinese emperor, murderer (Son of Sam), messenger, businessman, red-dressed woman, rabbi, golem, giant white rat, suited man flying over the plains, panther, fat traffic director, bear, people in dormitory beds, dragon enveloping a traffic jam – Wilson evoked a mind or memory in torment, replaying itself into oblivion. In addition to its parallels with Kafka's subject matter, this also pertained to Hess's fate as a Nazi war criminal incarcerated in Spandau Gaol with six others in 1947: prior to the Nuremberg Tribunal, doctors and psychiatrists had concluded that Hess was a psychopath, with paranoid delusions, suicidal tendencies in reaction to his failed flying mission to England, and a hysterical condition that led him to exaggerate his memory loss as a means of self-protection.

As his contribution to the 1987 Theater der Welt Festival in Stuttgart in July, Wilson directed Heiner Müller's 1981 play *Quartett* (based on the 1782 novel *Les Liaisons Dangereuses* by Choderlos de Laclos) in the small eighteenth-century court theater of Ludwigsburg Castle. Müller wrote for two characters, Merteuil and Valmont (a marquess and viscount, former lovers). Wilson extended the cast with three non-speaking parts, Old Man, Young Man, and Young Woman (juxtaposing one older and two voluptuously youthful bodies with those of the middle-aged decadents). He staged it as a spare and briskly moving chamber piece, underscoring the role-playing and sadomasochistic tone of the text with his props: a malevolent phallic symbol in the form of a tall steel chair frame; shoes used as fetishes; a black satin sofa with undulating female curves; a noose; the Young Woman in black mask, underwear, and high heels. (*Quartett* was produced in English at the American Repertory Theatre in Cambridge, Massachusetts, in 1988, with Lucinda Childs as Merteuil.)

In July Wilson created the installation piece *Memory of a Revolution* for the Galerie der Stadt, Stuttgart.

In collaboration with German playwright Tankred Dorst, Wilson made a new three-and-a-half hour work, *Parzival: From the Other Side of the Lake,* which premiered in Hamburg in September. Twenty-eight-year-old Christopher Knowles led a cast of fourteen, playing Parzival as a happy innocent in the leisure clothes of a modern youth: sweater, slacks, and sneakers.

The Rome section of *the CIVIL warS* received the American Theatre Wing Design award for noteworthy unusual effects; The Knee Plays received the Bessie Award, *Alcestis* received the French Critics Award for Best Foreign Play, *Hamletmachine* received the Berlin Festspiele Theatertreffen award.

1988
In March Wilson directed and co-choreographed (with Suzushi Hanayagi) a ballet for the first time. Working for the Paris Opéra Ballet (artistic director: Rudolph Nureyev) he chose the rarely performed 1911 scenic cantata *Le Martyre de Saint Sébastien* by Gabriele D'Annunzio and Claude Debussy. D'Annunzio likened it to a medieval mystery play, combining song, dance, acting, recitation, and tableau. In the original 1911 production and in Wilson's version Sébastien was danced by women (Ida Rubinstein and Sylvie Guillem, respectively).

Wilson added a slow, anxiety-ridden prologue, set on the deck of a luxury yacht such as D'Annunzio would have known. Furthermore, he omitted Debussy's choral music and provided barely enough dancing to satisfy traditional balletomanes. As a result of these changes, the piece elicited strong criticism in both Paris and New York (where it was performed at the Metropolitan Opera House in July). In a perceptive review, Dale Harris wrote: "Wilson has displaced D'Annunzio's sequential narrative with a series of dream visions, during the course of which the central matters of the saint's martyrdom and its ramifications are refracted through a number of different aesthetic points of view. No longer is the [preposterously flamboyant] text a means of characterization; it is simply one element in a complex assault upon the audience's powers of imaginative awareness, along with the music, the dance, and the spectacle... Much of Mr. Wilson's effectiveness as a purveyor of theatrical illusion derives from his radical disruptions of ordinary, perceived reality. [He] splits Sebastian into two characters: the potential martyr and the actual martyr. The first is a slim, athletic androgyne (Sylvie Guillem), the second an overweight and raddled old queen, dressed in tights, a dance belt, and the top half of a French sailor suit (Michael Denard). Taken together, these figures are a frank acknowledgement of the sanctimony and the prurience in D'Annunzio's original conception, as well as of the contradictory ways in which the saint has been viewed by succeeding generations. [In his purging Wilson] has substituted elements familiar from his other theatrical work: reiteration, ceremony, the prolongation of time ... But it is [his] often uncanny strokes of theatrical brilliance that give the production its luster, [as in] the moment when Sebastian the ephebe spurns the Emperor's advances and slashes the strings of the lute set before him, whereupon the sky turns indigo and the distant buildings of Rome glow incandescently. The best comes last: a vision of paradise blanched with radiance, in which a single crimson angel flames against the all-encompassing whiteness of sky, animals, vegetation, saints."[24]

In June Wilson designed and directed the jazz opera *Cosmopolitan Greetings* for the Hamburg State Opera. It was a dense, lively, and wide-ranging spectacle, within which several scenes focused on the life and death of Bessie Smith. Allen

Le Martyre de Saint Sébastien, Paris Opera Ballet, 1988.
Photos by Rodolphe Torette.

Ginsberg's poems were used as lyrics; George Gruntz, leader of the Big Band of North German Radio, wrote settings which ranged from blues to free-jazz; composer Rolf Liebermann, director of the Hamburg State Opera, wrote twelve-tone interludes for string ensemble; the performers included singer Dee Dee Bridgwater, trumpeter Don Cherry, and dancer Lutz Forster (of the Pina Bausch company).

For the Theater der Freien Volksbühne in West Berlin Wilson and David Byrne created *The Forest*, presenting themes from the ancient story of Gilgamesh, despotic ruler of the city of Uruk, and his rivalry and friendship with Enkidu, a hairy man who inhabits the natural world of animals. Gilgamesh, a representative of urban culture, appeared as a nineteenth-century prince of industrialization, and that century's most schizoid responses to nature and imagination, realism and romanticism, were evoked in references to Edgar Allen Poe's stories, *Silence – A Fable* and *Shadow – A Parable*. In this lavish four-hour production (structured in seven acts with three entractes) Heiner Müller and Darryl Pinckney contributed texts and Frida Parmegianni designed the costumes. The budget of $ 4 million was met largely by the city as part of the Berlin-Kulturstadt Europas 1988 festival. In his review Robert Brustein wrote: "[Those] who find the form or content of *The Forest* overly dense are rewarded by a wealth of dazzling and exquisitely executed dream images: ... factory workers laboring on huge ladders near massive gears as Gilgamesh smokes in his chair, attended by eerie domestics and a torpid lion; the golden Enkidu in his cave, accompanied by an armored knight, a figure in doublet and hose, a man cooking himself in a vat, and an outsized porcupine... The rock and ice landscapes of the concluding acts, where the two men join in battle with a dragon. Inadequate to encompass such intricate achievement, journalism can only salute it."[25]

Wilson received the Institute Honor from the American Institute of Architects (New York) and the Mondello Award for Theater (Palermo) for *Hamletmachine*.

1989
The Musée d'Orsay, Paris, commissioned Wilson to make a six-minute video tape work about Paul Cézanne's painting *La*

Suzushi Hanayagi in *La Femme à la Cafetière*, Musée d'Orsay, Paris, 1989.
Photo by Gérard Sergent.

Femme à la Cafetière, a work in the permanent collection. Suzushi Hanayagi was featured as the woman depicted by Cézanne.

Wilson made the video work *The Death of King Lear* as an independent production for the Spanish television series "The Art of Video."

In his second production at La Scala (in May) Wilson staged the premiere of Giacomo Manzoni's opera, *Doktor Faustus*, based on Thomas Mann's novel.

In June *De Materie*, a new opera by Wilson and the Dutch Minimalist composer Louis Andreissen, premiered for the Netherlands Opera at the Muziektheater Amsterdam, and was also performed in The Hague and Rotterdam.

Wilson was invited by President Mitterand to be the scenic director for the Paris gala concert on July 13, inaugurating the new Opéra Bastille. The evening event was televised as part of the national celebrations of the bicentennial of the French Revolution. Drawings for the stage designs, and Wilson's first large painting (based on one of the drawings), were exhibited at Galerie Yvon Lambert, Paris.

Robert Wilson and Jutta Lampe in rehearsals
for Orlando, Schaubühne Theater,
Berlin, 1989.
Photo by Ruth Walz.

In November Wilson created *Orlando,* a response to Virginia
Woolf's 1928 novel of the same name, at the Schaubühne am
Halleschen Ufer, Berlin. He commissioned a text from Darryl
Pinckney. In her fanciful biography of Orlando, a young
Elizabethan nobleman whose life spanned centuries and conti-
nents, Woolf snobbishly spoofed the British penchant for
historical novels and memoirs. During the Age of Enlighten-
ment, Orlando mysteriously changed sex and experienced the
rest of time – right up to 1928 – as a woman. The feminist
critique of Victorian culture in *Orlando* complemented Woolf's
hypothesis that the male and the female can coexist in one
individual. The program book for the Wilson/Pinckney *Orlando*
reprinted selections from Woolf's diaries to show extensive
connections between the novel and her life, including the way
in which she entwined the writing of it into her relationship
with Vita Sackville-West.

Surprisingly, in the theater where he created his *Death
Destruction and Detroit* extravaganzas, Wilson forsook the
novel's many instances of visual spectacle in favor of a sceni-
cally spare, two-hour monologue for actress Jutta Lampe. In
choosing to treat *Orlando* as a lonely woman's soliloquy he
made it easier to perceive the many voices implied by the text.
In her review, Maria Nadotti wrote: "Orlando's story swings
back and forth from the first-person [of the first act] to the
second-person of the middle act, where the transformation has
occurred, back to the first-person of the third and final act,
where Lady Orlando assumes, in the present, an identity that is
modified but all her own ... [Jutta Lampe] speaks without any
significant variation in gesture or vocabulary. While discretely
female movements prevail in him/her, they are for the most part
held on an ambiguously neutral plane... The passage from
male to female is accomplished by a quiet but brilliant
rhetorical device, with everything hinging on what is not shown
and what is left unsaid. A tree trunk (the old oak precious to
Woolf?) – metaphysical, abstract, completely symbolic, [and]
easily exchanged for a column or other architectural element –
descends like a mysterious deus ex machina, splitting the stage
into two equivalent and symmetrical parts. Orlando emerges
from behind the tree, transformed into Lady Orlando, but there
is nothing exceptional here, in what might otherwise have been
a coup de théatre. The transformation has simply occurred: a

subtle, ineffable event, simultaneously logical and bizarre. A delicate and mysterious balance, but not ambiguous, between a before and an after, between what is and what is no longer."[26]

In December Wilson staged Anton Chekhov's 1887–88 play *Swan Song* at the Kammerspiele Theater, Munich. In his *Village Voice* review, Marc Robinson wrote, "*Swan Song* pitches Svetlovidov, an aging second-rate actor, in a dark theater long after the evening's performance has ended. [He] waxes maudlin about his past glories for the benefit of an old prompter, Ivanitsch… In Wilson's setting the two look sad and abandoned. Soaring walls dwarf them and their loneliness… Even the smallest moments in Wilson's score contribute to the pervasive feeling of regal disintegration. The Greek pillar sitting upstage suggests a lost splendor, much like the old actor himself, and now stands just as foolish and alone, willfully anachronistic and still radiating self-importance. Movement is not always as soporific as in much Wilson; instead it is anxious and uncertain, full of grand gestures that collapse into restless twitching. *[Swan Song]* looks and sounds like one of Wilson's most personal pieces. The small scale helps… Wilson himself edges into view, working out obsessions, completing an exercise that seems to have inscrutable, private significance. At times the process becomes painfully intense. [What in a larger work] might have looked like ceremony … shows itself as visceral suffering – all the more persuasive for the precision with which Wilson reveals it."[27]

Wilson founded RW Work Ltd. to produce limited editions of furniture and sculpture fabricated by Editions Dosi Delfini.

New York Public Library named Wilson Lion of the Performing Arts; Furniture and drawings from *Parzifal* and *Hamletmachine* awarded Great Prize at Sao Paulo Biennial; *Doktor Faustus* received Italian Theater Critics best production of the year award (Milan, Italy).

1990
In collaboration with William Burroughs, who wrote the text, and Tom Waits, who composed songs, Wilson created *The Black Rider: The Casting of the Magic Bullets* for the Thalia Theater, Hamburg, in March. Comic, lively, and "Germanic," this pastiche of operetta, cabaret, and rock concerts presented

William S. Burroughs and Robert Wilson, 1990.
Photo by Elisabeth Henrichs.

the tragic tale *Der Freischütz,* by August Apel and Friedrich Laun, the 1810 text that inspired Weber's opera of the same name.) This production traveled to Vienna in June, and Paris in October. It was recorded for Austrian television by ORF in cooperation with Thalia Theater.

In April Wilson created *Room for Salome* for the group exhibition *Energieen* (Stedelijk Museum, Amsterdam): two glass staffs and four pieces of seating furniture originally designed for his 1987 production of *Salome* were grouped in a darkened room on a large sloping rectangle of dried earth; spoken excerpts from the *Salome* texts (in German and in English) created a sound environment.

Wilson produced *King Lear* (an edited version of Shakespeare's text) for Schauspiel Frankfurt in May. Eighty-year-old actress Marianne Hoppe played Lear. Drawings related to the work were shown at Kunsthalle Schirn, Frankfurt.

Revival of Wilson's production of Gluck's *Alceste* Lyric Opera of Chicago, September

Alceste Drawings and Furniture/Sculpture
An exhibition at Feigen Incorporated, Chicago, September

1991

Robert Wilson's Vision, organized by the Museum of Fine Arts, Boston, February (also shown at the Contemporary Arts Museum, Houston, and the San Francisco Museum of Modern Art).

Productions Planned for 1991

When We Dead Awaken (based on Henrik Ibsen's last play, written in 1899)
American Repertory Theatre, Cambridge, Mass. February (traveling to the Alley Theater, Houston, Texas, May)
Parsifal, by Richard Wagner
Hamburg State Opera, March (traveling to the Houston Grand Opera, February 1992)

Revival of Wilson/Manzoni *Doktor Faustus*
Frankfurt Opera, April

The Magic Flute, by Wolfgang Amadeus Mozart
Opéra Bastille, Paris, June

Lohengrin, by Richard Wagner
Zurich Opera, September

Exhibition of furniture, sculpture, and videos at Centre Pompidou, Paris, November

Don Giovanni, by Wolfgang Amadeus Mozart
Deutsche Oper, Berlin, November

Notes

1. Byrd Hoffman, "The King of Spain," in *New American Plays* vol. 3 (New York, 1970), pp. 246–47.

2. Stefan Brecht, *The Theatre of Visions: Robert Wilson* (Frankfurt, 1978), p. 14.

3. David Bradby and David Williams, *Directors' Theatre* (London, 1988), p. 225.

4. Ellen Stodolsky, "New Dance/Theater: Theater that Moves," *Dance Magazine,* April 1974, p. 51.

5. Jill Johnston's "Dance Journal," *Village Voice,* 7 Nov. 1968, quoted in Brecht, *Theatre of Visions,* p. 37.

6. Stephen Smoliar, "Byrd Hoffman School of Byrds, Anderson Theatre," *Dance Magazine,* Mar. 1969, p. 93.

7. Richard Foreman, *Village Voice,* 1 Jan. 1970, quoted in Brecht, *Theatre of Visions,* pp. 425–27.

8. John Perreault, "Art: Trying Harder," *Village Voice,* 1 Jan. 1970, p. 16.

9. Louis Aragon, "Lettre ouverte à André Breton sur *Le Regard du Sourd,* l'art, la science, et la liberté," *Les Lettres Françaises* (June 2, 1971) quoted in Brecht, *Theatre of Visions,* pp. 433–438 [author's translation].

10. Basil Langton, "Journey to Ka Mountain," *Drama Review,* June 1973), p. 53.

11. Edwin Denby, "You Never Heard of a Silent Opera?" *New York Times,* 9 Dec. 1973, p. 10.

12. T. E. Kalem, "Labyrinthine Dream," *Time,* 31 Dec. 1973, p. 47.

13. Wilson quoted in Bill Simmer, "Robert Wilson and Therapy," *Drama Review,* Mar. 1976, p. 109.

14. Laurence Shyer, *Robert Wilson and His Collaborators* (New York, 1989), p. 90.

15. Arnold Aronson, "Wilson/Knowles' "The $ Value of Man,'" *Drama Review* (Sept. 1975), pp. 106–110.

16. Robert Brustein, "Theater in the Age of Einstein: The Crack in the Chimney," *New York Times,* 1978. Reprinted in *Critical Moments: Reflection on Theatre and Society, 1973–1979* (New York 1980) pp. 120–21.

17. Robert Wilson "...I thought I was hallucinating," *Drama Review* Dec. 1977, p. 76.

18. Luis O. Arata, "Dreamscapes and other Reconstructions: The Theatre of Robert Wilson," *Kansas Quarterly* 12 (Fall 1980), p. 84.

19. "*Death Destruction & Detroit* in Berlin," *Performing Arts Journal* 1 (1979) pp. 3–4.

20. Craig Owens, "Robert Wilson: Tableaux," Art in America, Nov. 1980, p. 114.

21. Warrilow quoted in Shyer, *Wilson and his Collaborators,* p. 20.

22. John Rockwell, "Opera: 'Médée' paired with 'Medea' in Lyons, *New York Times,* Nov. 1, 1984, p. C19.

23. Elinor Fuchs, "Robert Wilson's 'Alcestis': A Classic for the '80s" *Village Voice,* July 29, 1986, pp. 36–40.

24. Dale Harris, "Paris Opera Ballet: Robert Wilson's 'Le Martyre,'" *Wall Street Journal* (July 12, 1988), p. 30.

25. "Robert Brustein On Theater," *New Republic* (Jan. 2, 1989).

26. Maria Nadotti, "On Robert Wilson's *Orlando,*" *Artforum* 28 (Feb. 1990), pp. 27–28.

27. Marc Robinson, "Wilson Plus Chekhov: The Master of Detachment Meets the Master of Melancholy," *Village Voice* (Apr. 4, 1990), p. 102.

SELECTED BIBLIOGRAPHY
Compiled by Virginia Abblitt

Monographs

Brecht, Stefan. *The Theater of Visions:* Robert Wilson. Frankfurt, 1979.

Donker, Janny. *The President of Paradise: A Traveller's Account of the CIVIL warS*. Translated by Cor Blok and Janny Donker. Amsterdam, 1985.

Quadri, Franco. *Il Teatro di Robert Wilson*. Venice, 1976.

Shyer, Laurence. *Robert Wilson and His Collaborators*. New York, 1989.

Stearns, Robert. *Robert Wilson: From a Theater of Images*. [Includes essay by John Rockwell, "Robert Wilson's Stage Works: Originality and Influences" and reprints Calvin Tompkins's *New Yorker* profile of Wilson.] Cincinnati, 1980.

Articles, Essays, Reviews

Aragon, Louis. "On Robert Wilson's *Deafman Glance*." Translated by Linda Moses. *Performing Arts Journal*. (Spring 1976), 3–7.

Arata, Luis O. "Dreamscapes and Other Reconstructions: The Theatre of Robert Wilson." *Kansas Quarterly* 12 (Fall 1980), 73–86.

Armstrong, Gordon S. "Images in the Interstice: The Phenomenal Theater of Robert Wilson." *Modern Drama* 31 (1988), 571 587.

Aronson, Arnold. "Wilson/Knowles': *The $ Value of Man*." *The Drama Review* 19 (September 1975), 106–110.

Barracks, Barbara. "Einstein on the Beach." *Artforum* 15 (March 1977), 31–36.

Barnes, Clive. "Must There Be A Story?" [*Deafman Glance*] *New York Times* (March 14, 1971, sec. D), 5.

Bly, Mark. "Notes on Robert Wilson's *Medea*." *Theater* 12 (Summer/Fall 1981), 65–68.

Brustein, Robert. "Theatre in the Age of Einstein: The Crack in the Chimney," 107–123. In *Critical Moments: Reflection on Theatre & Society*. [Reprint of 1978 essay] New York, 1980.

"Advanced Machines" [*Hamletmachine*]. *New Republic* (June 16, 1986), 27–29.

The Byrd Hoffman School of Byrds. "Textes, images, gravures, dessins, notes de travail sur les spectacles de la Compagnie." *Cahiers Renaud Barrault* 81–82 (1972).

Michel Corvin. "A Propos de deux Spectacles de Robert Wilson: Essai de Lecture Sémiologique. *Cahiers Renaud Barrault* 77 (1971).

Curiger, Bice and Jacqueline Burckhardt. "The Weight of a Grain of Dust." *Parkett* 16 (1988), 111–21.

Deak, Frantisek. "Robert Wilson." *The Drama Review* 18 (June 1974), 67–73.

Denby, Edwin. "You Never Heard of a Silent Opera?" *New York Times* (December 9, 1973, sec. 2), 10.

Fairbrother, Trevor. "Stretch-out, Robert Wilson's *Einstein Chair*." *Parkett* 16 (1988), 78–82.

Faust, Wolfgang Max. "Tagtraum und Theater." *Sprache im Technischen Zeitalter* 69 (January-March 1979), 30–58.

Finter, Helga. "Experimental Theatre and Semiology of Theatre: The Theatricalization of Voice." *Modern Drama* 26 (1983), 501–517.

Flakes, Susan. "Robert Wilson's *Einstein on the Beach*." *The Drama Review* 20 (December 1976), 69–82.

Fuchs, Elinor, ed. "The PAJ Casebook: Robert Wilson's *Alcestis*." *Performing Arts Journal* 28 (Summer 1986). [Includes statements by Laurie Anderson, John Conklin, Diane D'Aquila, Suzushi Hanayagi, Tom Kamm, Hans Peter Kuhn, Mark Oshima, Paul Rudd, Jennifer Tipton, and Heiner Müller's text: "Description of a Picture/Explosion of a Memory," translated by Carl Weber.]

"Robert Wilson's *Alcestis*, A Classic for the '80s." *Village Voice* (July 29, 1986), 38–40.

Grandjean, Christine. "Great Day in the Morning." *Parkett* 16 (1988), 98–103.

Harris, Melissa. "Robert Wilson" [*Einstein* at the Brooklyn Academy of Music]. *Flash Art* 121 (March 1985), 44.

Henrichs, Benjamin. "Die ästhetische Riesenmaus" [Death, Destruction, and Detroit II]. *Die Zeit*. March 6, 1987.

"Der bunte Reiter." [The Black Rider]. *Die Zeit*. May 4, 1987.

"Die Nacht der Könige" [The CIVIL warS]. *Die Zeit*. January 26, 1984, 33–34.

Howell, John. "Forum: What a Legend Becomes" [*Einstein* restaged]. *Artforum* 23 (March 1985), 90.

"Robert Wilson and David Byrne, *The Knee Plays*." *Artforum* 25 (March 1987), 131.

"Robert Wilson: *Quartet*." *Artforum* 26 (May 1988), 151–152.

Johnen, Jörg. "Der Sinn gehört der Sphäre der Selbstbedienung, Saft Wilson; *Curious George*, Knowles/ Wilson Fünfter Dialog." *Theater Heute* 9 (September 1980), 28–29.

Johnston, Jill. "Family Spectacles." *Art in America* 74 (December 1986), 94–106.

Kauffmann, Stanley. "Robert Wilson" [*The Life and Times of Joseph Stalin*]. *New Republic* 171 (January 5, 1974), 16, 33–34.

"The $ Value of Man." *New Republic* 172 (May 31, 1975), 20, 33.

Kertess, Klaus. "In Robert Wilson's Forest." *Parkett* 16 (1988), 56–61.

Langton, Basil. "Journey to Ka Mountain." *The Drama Review* 17 (June 1973), 48–57.

Larson, Kay. "Robert Wilson." *Art News* 77 (March 1978), 172.

Lehmann, Hans-Thies. "Robert Wilson, Scenographer." *Parkett* 16 (1988), 44–50.

Levy, Ellen. "Robert Wilson: Theater History, Theater as History." *Parkett* 16 (1988), 66–69.

Lipman, Samuel. "*Einstein's* Long March to Brooklyn." *The New Criterion* 3 (February 1985), 15–24.

Lorber, Richard. [Review of *Patio* … at Cherry Lane Theatre] *Artforum* 16 (September 1977), 77.

[Review of Wilson's sculptures at Multiples/Goodman Gallery]. *Artforum* 16 (February 1978), 64–65.

Marranca, Bonnie. "Robert Wilson, the Avant-Garde and the Audience." *New York Arts Journal* (Spring 1977), 19–20.

"The Forest as Archive: Wilson and Interculturism." *Performing Arts Journal* 11/12 (Summer 1989), 36–44.

Maurin, Frédéric. "Robert Wilson: Un Temps Venu D'Ailleurs." *Art-Press* [Numero special: théâtre] (1989) 208–211.

Munk, Erika. "And Thereby Hangs a Tail." [*Dialog/Curious George*] Village Voice (July 2, 1980), 65.

Müller, Heiner. "Reflections on Post-Modernism." *New German Critique* 6 (Winter 1979), 55–57.

Nadotti, Maria. "Robert Wilson's *Orlando.*" *Artforum* 28 (February 1990), 27–28.

Owens, Craig. "*Einstein on the Beach:* The Primacy of Metaphor." *October* 4 (Fall 1978), 21–32.

"Robert Wilson: Tableaux." *Art in America* 68 (November 1980), 114–117.

Quadri, Franco. "Robert Wilson: It's About Time." *Artforum* 23 (October 1984), 76–82.

Rainer, Yvonne; Monk, Meredith; and King, Kenneth. "R.E.: Croce." *Live* (1980), 18–22.

Rogoff, Gordon. "*Hamletmachine.*" *Performing Arts Journal* 28 (Summer 1986), 54–57.

Rouse, John. "Robert Wilson, Texts and History: *CIVIL warS*, German Part." *Theater* 16 (Fall/Winter 1984), 68–74.

"Structuring Stories: Robert Wilson's *Alcestis.*" *Theater* (Fall/Winter 1986), 56–59.

Shapiro, David. "Notes on *Einstein on the Beach.*" *New York Arts Journal* (Spring 1977), 21–22.

Simmer, Bill. "Robert Wilson and Therapy." *The Drama Review* 20 (March 1976), 99–110.

Taubin, Amy. "Talking Through Customs at the Video Border." *Alive* (September/October 1982), 30–32.

Tomkins, Calvin. "Time to Think: Profile of Robert Wilson." *The New Yorker.* (January 13, 1975), 38–62.

Trilling, Ossia. "Robert Wilson's Ka Mountain and Guardenia Terrace." *The Drama Review* 17 (June 1973), 33–47.

Tucker, Carll. "An Entirely Unfamiliar Human Way of Perceiving the World." *Village Voice* (March 24, 1975), 71–72.

Interviews and Statements by Wilson

Alenikoff, Frances. "Scenario: A Talk with Robert Wilson." *Dancescope* 10 (Fall/Winter 1975/76), 11–21.

Brody, Jacqueline. "Robert Wilson, Performance on Paper." *Print Collector's Newsletter* 16 (September- October 1985), 117–124.

Frick, Tom. "A Conversation with Robert Wilson." *Art New England* 6 (June 1985), 4,20.

Hoffman, Byrd [Robert Wilson]. Production Notes on *The King of Spain.*" *New American Plays* vol. 3 (1970), 243–272.

Lesschaeve, Jacqueline. "Robert Wilson, Responses." *Tel Quel* 71/73 (Autumn 1977), 217–225.

Lotringer, Sylvere. "Robert Wilson Interview." *Semiotexte* 3 (1978), 20–27.

Mignet, Dorine. "Room for Salome. Interview with Robert Wilson," in Energieen (exh. cat.). Stedelijk Museum Amsterdam, 1990, pp 112–113.

Mousseau, Jeff. "Robert Wilson." [*The Forest*] *Splash* (April 1989), n.p.

Prikker, Bertel Thorn. "I Just Want To Be Normal." *Ricochet* (Autumn 1987), 31–37.

Shyer, Laurence. "Robert Wilson: the CIVIL warS and After." *Theater* 16 (Summer/Fall 1985), 72–80.

Shyer, Laurence. "Robert Wilson: Current Projects." *Theater* 14 (Summer/Fall 1983), 83–98.

Exhibition and Performance Catalogs
(arranged chronologically)

Festival d'Automne a Paris. *A Letter for Queen Victoria: An Opera in Four Acts* [Texts by Robert Wilson, Stephan Brecht, Christopher Knowles, Cindy Lubar, James Neu; calligraphy by Cindy Lubar]. 1974.

Musée Galliera, Paris. *Robert Wilson: Dessins et Sculptures* [Texts by Paul Schmidt, Robert Wilson, Mary Peer, Christopher Knowles]. 1974.

Alliata, Vicky, ed. *Einstein on the Beach* [essay on Wilson by Vicky Alliata, essay on Philip Glass by Richard Foreman]. New York [1976].

Galerie Folker Skulima, Berlin. *Skulpturen von Robert Wilson* [Essays by Cindy Lubar and Roland H. Wiegenstein]. 1978.

Städtische Gallerie, Lenbachhaus, Munich. *The Golden Windows* [Wilson's text and drawings for the play and essays by Michael Wachsmann and Gabriele Lohnert]. 1982.

Belloli, Andrea P. A., ed. *the CIVIL warS: Drawings, Models, and Documentation* [essays by Al Nodal, Wim Beeren, Lori J. Starr, Richard Stayton, and annotated storyboards by Wilson]. Otis Art Institute of Parsons School of Design. Los Angeles, 1984.

American Repertory Theatre, Cambridge, Mass. *Robert Wilson: the CIVIL warS* [Interview with Wilson by Jonathan Marks, telegram to Wilson from Heiner Müller, and excerpts from the script]. 1985.

Rose, Bernice. *New Works on Paper 3*. Museum of Modern Art, New York, 1985.

Galerie Fred Jahn, Munich. *Robert Wilson: Die lithographischen Zyklen, 1984-1986: Medea, Parsifal, Alceste* [Introduction by Fred Jahn.] 1986.

Galerie Harold Behm, Hamburg. *Robert Wilson: Parzival.* [Essay by Jörg Krichbaum.] 1987.

Reinhardt, Brigitte. *Robert Wilson: Erinnerung an eine Revolution; Environment*. Galerie der Stadt Stuttgart. Stuttgart, 1987.

Schaubühne am Lehniner Platz, Berlin. *Robert Wilson: Death Destruction & Detroit II*. 1987.

Theater der Freien Volksbühne Berlin- Kulturstadt Europas, Berlin. *The Forest* [statements by Wilson, Heiner Muller, David Byrne and Darryl Pinckney.] 1988.

Annemarie Verna Galerie, Zürich. *Orlando* [essay by Darryl Pinckney, drawings by Wilson]. 1989.

Münchner Kammerspiele Schauspielhaus. *Schwanengesang* [Anton Chekhov's play and Wilson's drawings and furniture]. Frankfurt am Main, 1989.

Schaubühne am Lehniner Platz, Berlin. *Orlando* [diary and letters by Virginia Woolf and drawings by Robert Wilson]. Frankfurt am Main, 1989.

Thalia Theater, Hamburg. *The Black Rider: The Casting of the Magic Bullets* [drawings by Wilson and William Burroughs; songs by Tom Waits; texts by William Burroughs, August Apel and Friedrich Laun, Thomas de Quincey, Otto von Graben zum Stein]. 1990.

Schauspiel Frankfurt. *William Shakespeare: König Lear.* [Drawings and furniture by Robert Wilson]. 1990.

Hans Peter Kuhn.
Photo by David Slama.

1952
Born in Kiel, West Germany
After high school, sang and played in several rock and roll
bands

1975—79
Worked as sound engineer at the Schaubühne am Halleschen
Ufer, Berlin

1978
Sound engineer and editor for Adolf Winkelmann's *Die
Abfahrer* [On the Move]

1979
Sound designer:
    Robert Wilson's *Death Destruction & Detroit*, Schaubühne am
    Halleschen Ufer, Berlin
    Peter Goedel's documentary film *Talentprobe* [Talent
    Audition]

1980
Sound engineer for Dieter Dorn's production of *Danton's Tod*
[Danton's Death], Kammerspiele, Munich
Sound engineer and editor for Adolph Winkelmann's film *Jede
Menge Kohle* [Lots of Bills to Pay]

1981
Sound artist:
    Luc Bondy's *Macbeth*, Schauspielhaus, Cologne
    Robert Wilson's *The Man in the Raincoat*, Schauspielhaus,
    Cologne

1982
Sound performance of *Jenseits von Reden* [Beyond Talking],
Munich, Berlin, Frankfurt, Freiburg
Soundscore for Peter Goedel's film *Rückkehr zu den Sternen*
[Return to the Stars]
Sound artist for Robert Wilson's *Golden Windows*, Munich

1982—85
Sound artist for the Dutch, German, Japanese, French, and
Italian sections of Robert Wilson's *the CIVIL warS*

1984
Sound engineer for Peter Zadek's production of *Ghetto*, Freie
Volksbühne, Berlin; Deutsches Schauspielhaus, Hamburg
Sound installations:
    Das Audio-Cafe, in group exhibition *Kunst und Medien* (with
    Benoit Maubrey), Staatliche Kunsthalle, Berlin
    end of transmission, in group exhibition *Belle-Vue* (with
    Eberhard Kramer), Kreuzlingen, Switzerland
    Die Audio-Badewanne [The Audio-Bathtub], in group
    exhibition *Aussenseite-Innenseite* (with Benoit Maubrey),
    Kutscherhaus, Berlin

HANS PETER KUHN
Compiled by Peter Barr

Radio work, *Rush Hour*, Südwestfunk, Sender Freies Berlin, Saarländischer Rundfunk, Radio Bremen, Bayerischer Rundfunk

Performance of *Automusik*, Die Anweisung, Yorckbrücken, Berlin

1985

Sound artist for Robert Wilson's *The Golden Windows*, Brooklyn Academy of Music, New York

Performances:

Jenseits von Reden, New York

Sprechende Kleider [Audio Uniforms], Berlin, Munich, Lisbon

Installations:

Menschen als Medien [Men as Media], solo exhibition at Galerie NoName, Berlin

The Box, group exhibition *Berlin* (with Benoit Maubrey), Kulturzentrum Gasteig München, Munich, Art-Of-Peace-Biennale, Hamburg

Founding member of free radio station "Die Audionauten" in Berlin

1986

Sound artist:

Robert Wilson's *Alcestis*, American Repertory Theatre, Cambridge, Massachusetts

Luc Bondy's *Die Fremdenführerin* [The Female Visitor's Guide] Schaubühne am Halleschen Ufer, Berlin

Claus Peymann's *Der Theatermacher* [The Theater Manager], Burgtheater, Vienna, Austria

Michael Braun's *Das Totenfloss* [The Death Raft], Schauspielhaus, Düsseldorf

Radio work, *Tasso. Ein Torso*, RIAS (Korredat), Berlin

Live radio concert *Sprechende Kleider*, Ars Electronica, Linz, Austria

Performances:

Sprechende Kleider, Linz, Austria

Jenseits von Reden, Fünf Hören [Hear Five], and *Sprechende Kleider*, Pittsburgh, Pennsylvania, and Boston, Massachusetts

1987

Sound artist for Robert Wilson:

Death, Destruction & Detroit II, Schaubühne am Halleschen Ufer, Berlin

Alceste, Schauspielhaus, Stuttgart

Installations:

Casa Grande (part 1), in group exhibition KunstTage (with Eberhard Kramer), Galerie Vayhinger Moggingen

Casa Grande (part 2), (with Eberhard Kramer), NBK-exhibition, Haus am Waldsee, Berlin

Glashafen [Glass Harbor], solo exhibition commissioned by the Internationalen Bauausstellung, Behala-Hafen, Berlin

Performances:

Tripod, Die Anweisung, Berlin

Guitar Monkeys, Space Night Show, HdK, Berlin

Plakat-Anschlag [Poster Display/Attacking a Poster], S-Bhf Schöneberg, Berlin

1988

Sound engineer for Claus Peymann's production of *Der Sturm* [The Tempest], Burgtheater, Vienna, Austria

Sound artist for Robert Wilson:

Le Martyre de Saint Sébastien, Opera de Paris; Metropolitan Opera, New York

Cosmopolitan Greetings, Hamburgische Staatsoper

The Forest, Freie Volksbühne, Berlin; Brooklyn Academy of Music, New York

Installations:

Fassungslos [Speechless], solo exhibition at Laden für Nichts, Berlin; group exhibiton *Jahresausstellung des Deutschen Künstlerbund*, Württembergischer Kunstverein, Stuttgart

Essen und Hören [Eating and Hearing], solo exhibition for *Krakatau Jugendwerkstatt* under the aegis of E 88, Berlin

Achtundacht (für Irene) [Eight-and-Eight (for Irene)], solo exhibition at S-Bhf, Westkreuz; included in the group exhibition *Statmusik* under the aegis of E 88, Berlin Statmusik

Als das Verwünschen noch geholfen hat [As It Has Cursed, Yet It Has Helped], in group exhibition *Klanginstallationen auf der Ars Electronica*, Linz, Austria

The Golem, in group exhibition Europäisches Medienkunst-
festival (with Simon Biggs), Osnabrück; and at Cleveland
Gallery, Middlesbrough, England

Radio work 25 Rauschen [25 Rustling Noises], Radio 100,
Berlin

Performance of Fünf Hören, Ars Electronica, Linz, Austria

1989

Installations:
Vor Tagesanbruch [Before Daybreak], in group exhibition
First Macrophon Festival, Club der 13 Musen, Stettin, Poland

In Fluss [In Flux] and Die Drei Affen [The Three Monkeys], in
group exhibition Ulrich Eller und Hans Peter Kuhn,
Gesellschaft fur Aktuelle Kunst, Bremen

Sound artist for dance works:
Suspect Terrain, with Dana Reitz, Steve Paxton, Laurie
Booth, Polly Motley, Pepsico Summerfare, New York. (In
1990, Kuhn won a Bessie Award for his contribution.)

Music for Americium 225 '89, a solo performance by Suzushi
Hanayagi, Tokyo

Sound artist for Luc Bondy's Die Zeit und Das Zimmer [The
Time and The Room], Schaubühne am Halleschen Ufer, Berlin

Sound artist and composer for Robert Wilson's Orlando,
Schaubühne am Halleschen Ufer, Berlin

1990

Sound artist for dance works:
Well Known Worlds, with Laurie Booth, ICA, London
Americium '31–90, with Suzushi Hanayagi, jean-jean-
theatre, Tokyo
Spatial Decay, with Laurie Booth, The Place, London and
Riverside Studio, London

Sound engineer for Claus Peymann's Das Spiel von Fragen
[The Play of Questions], Burgtheater, Vienna, Austria

Sound artist:
Robert Wilson's King Lear, Schauspiel, Frankfurt
Thomas Brasch's Liebe Machte Tod [Love, Power, Death],
Schillertheater, Berlin

Radio play, Stille [Silence] (with Sarbine Pochhammer)

Projected for 1991

Installations:
Wetterleuchten [Lightning], Berlin
The Pier, commissioned by the New York International
Festival of The Arts, New York, New York

Sound installation for the exhibition, Robert Wilson's Vision,
exhibition organized by the Museum of Fine Arts, Boston

Sound artist for Robert Wilson's When We Dead Awaken
(Ibsen), American Repertory Theatre, Cambridge

Installation, The Pier, commissioned by the New York International Festival of The Arts, New York

Selected Bibliography

Books and Articles

John Calhoun, "Creating an Audio Environment," Theatre
Crafts Magazine, January 1989

Janny Donker, The President of Paradise: A Traveler's Account
of the CIVIL warS, Amsterdam, 1985

Elinor Fuchs, "Hans Peter Kuhn: Audio Environment,"
Performing Arts Journal, 28 (1986)

Laurence Shyer, Robert Wilson and his Collaborators, New
York, 1989

Catalogues

"Ars Electronica 1986," Linz, 1986
"Ars Electronica 1988," Linz, 1988
"Aussenseite-Innenseite," Kutscherhaus, Berlin, 1984
"Benoit Maubrey – Die Audio Gruppe," Berlin, 1990
"Biennale des Friedens," Kunstverein Hamburg, 1985
"Die Anweisung," Berlin, 1987
"Die Stimme in der Kunst," Bad Rappenau, 1989
"Jahresausstellung 1988," Deutscher Künstlerbund, Stuttgart,
1988
"Klanginstallationen – Ulrich Eller/Hans Peter Kuhn,"
Gesellschaft für Aktuelle Kunst, Bremen, 1989
"KunstTage," Galerie Vayhinger, Radolfzell, 1987
"Macrophon," Ruine der Künste Berlin und Pro Arte Acustica
Stettin, Poland, 1989
"Quergalerie im Eisstadion," Berlin, 1985
"Sprechende Kleider – Menschen als Medien," Berlin, 1985

THE NIGHT BEFORE THE DAY: Score by Hans Peter Kuhn

1. Entrance   11'50"

Wind, chorus sound, whisper:	*the CIVIL warS*, Rotterdam
Birdsounds (Jutta Lampe):	*Orlando*, Berlin
Water dripping:	*The Forest*, Berlin

2. Room I   14'47"

Cleaning dishes:	*Death Destruction and Detroit II*, Berlin
Breaking and falling glasses:	*Orlando*, Berlin
Dance class:	Rehearsals for *the CIVIL warS*, Rome
Cobblestone layers in Berlin:	*Le Martyre de Saint Sébastien*, Paris
Text 90 (Robert Wilson):	*The Man in the Raincoat*, Cologne
Two minutes laughing (Maria Nicklisch):	*The Golden Windows*, Munich

3. Room II   4'33"

Six harpsichords playing simultaneously:	*Orlando*, Berlin
Screaming (Cindy Lubar).	*The Life and Times of Joseph Stalin*

4. Room III   15'37"

Melody "Machinery":	*the CIVIL warS*, Cologne
Man whistling:	*King Lear*, Frankfurt
Ringing telephone:	*Death, Destruction, and Detroit I*, Berlin
Boatswain whistle:	*King Lear*, Frankfurt
Dog barking:	*Alcestis*, Cambridge, Massachusetts
Altered cymbal sound:	*Orlando*, Berlin
Text (Marianne Hoppe):	*King Lear*, Frankfurt

5. The Space Ship   0'20"

All additional parts were made especially for this exhibition.

All compositions by Hans Peter Kuhn, lyrics by Robert Wilson, William Shakespeare.

HM HM HM HM HM OK OK OK OK OK THERE THERE THE OA OA OA OA
HM HM HM HM OK OK OK OK HAT HM THERE THE OA OA OA HM H
HM HM HM OK OK OK HAT HM THERE THE OA OA HM HM

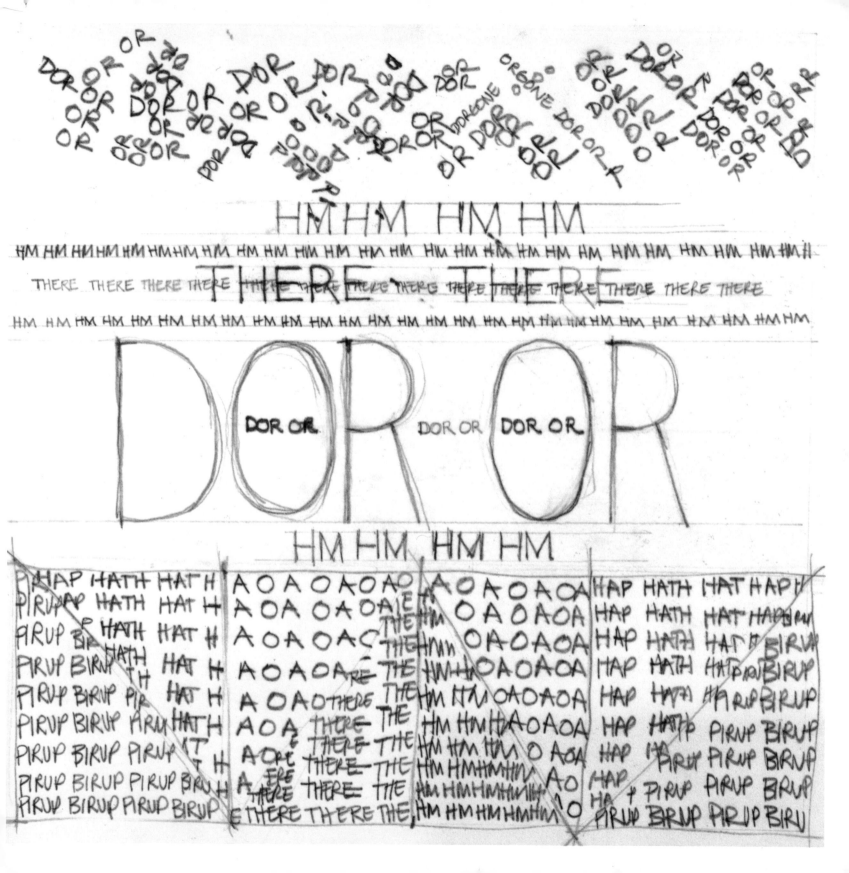

Errata: Robert Wilson's Vision

page 13, paragraph 2, delete third sentence

page 17, line 2, for "opprobious" read "opprobrious"

page 50, drawing is printed upside down

page 109, line 36, for "Byrd" read "Bird"

page 141, column 2, lines 8 and 9, for "Kramer" read "Krämer"
          line 8, for "Moggingen" read "Möggingen"
          line 35, for "Statmusik" read "Stattmusik"

page 142, column 1, line 32, for "von" read "vom"
          line 36, for "Machte" read "Macht"
          line 38, for "Sarbine" read "Sabine"